Co

Secrets

Of

Highly Successful People
Keys to Launching A Great Life

Lindy Schneider
and
Tom L. Schneider

Peaks Publishing Inc
www.PeaksPublishing.com

Names: Schneider, Lindy, author. | Schneider, Tom L., 1953- author.
Title: College secrets of highly successful people : keys to launching a great life / Lindy Schneider and Tom L. Schneider.
Description: [Littleton, Colorado] : Peaks Publishing Inc, [2020] | Interest age level: High school and up. | Includes bibliographical references and index.
Identifiers: ISBN 9780984038558
Subjects: LCSH: College students--Conduct of life. | Student activities. | Vocational guidance. | Successful people--Biography. | LCGFT: Biographies.
Classification: LCC LB3605 .S36 2020 | DDC 378.1/98--dc23

Summary: True stories of what celebrities, CEOs and other highly successful people did while in college to launch their careers with tips for college students on how to create their own success.

ISBN: 978-0-9840385-5-8

Bulk Sales: Bulk purchases of this book are available at special discounts. For more information, contact us at:

SpSales@PeaksPublishing.com

Cover Illustration: Aubrey Blankenship

Printed in the United States of America
Published by Peaks Publishing Inc

Praise for *College Secrets of Highly Successful People*

"Success after college is not assured by simply getting a degree. **College Secrets of Highly Successful People** reveals the secrets that celebrities, CEOs, billionaires, and even presidents used to launch their careers. Read this book to learn exactly what a student needs to know to find success in their own life and career and deliver the necessary return on investment for today's increasingly expensive college education."
— Beth V. Walker, author of *Never Pay Retail for College*

"We recommend **College Secrets of Highly Successful People** for students about to head to college, those in college, or those who are taking a different path. Everyone can not only benefit from the book, but will enjoy reading it."
— Vicki Nelson, CollegeParentCentral.com

"You can hope for success or seize it by following what other successful people have done. **College Secrets** is a must read if you want to make sure you get your money's worth out of a college education."
— Heidi Ganahl, University Regent

"**College Secrets of Highly Successful People** should be required reading for all students. This book provides thought-provoking insight and encourages personal evaluation. As my son dives into his college career, I'm thankful he'll have this tool available to him as a guide."
— Pam Ortiz, parent of college student

"I intended to skim this book before giving it to my grandson who is about to start college. However, I kept stopping to read one fascinating vignette after another. I highly recommend this book to anyone trying to make sense of what it really takes to have a successful life."
— Laurie Weiss, grandparent

BONUS: A Free Gift for You!

As a "thank you" for purchasing this book Tom and I would like to give you a FREE *College Secrets* video training. We will reveal some of the myths you might have heard about college and offer concrete steps you should take to get the best ROI on your college investment.

You will also learn some simple steps you can take that will give you a distinct advantage over other college students and set you on the path to a happy, successful life.

If you are currently attending college, planning on attending or love someone who is in college or college bound, watch this valuable FREE video training to start you on your own path to success. Go to:

www.AmericasCollegeAdvisors.com/FreeTraining

Also, look for other free bonuses throughout the book to help you implement the success secrets revealed in the following chapters.

Contents

Introduction

Whether you are a college bound student, or you love one, this book will give you the keys to open the door to a successful life. You are about to peek inside the personal lives of famous celebrities, CEOs, billionaires and former presidents to discover what they did while in college that launched their careers. We will also introduce you to other highly successful people whose names you won't recognize and tell you what they did as well.

We have interviewed and researched entrepreneurs, millionaires and others to find the secrets that they used while they were just college students to draw fame, fortune and life-long friendships into their lives. Now we are revealing the secrets we discovered to YOU!

People often ask Tom and me how we chose the people to showcase in this book. The world is filled with successful people for you to admire, but we looked for people who did things while enrolled in college that you could imitate.

There are hidden opportunities that can be accessed by college students that attract future success. Many of these opportunities are available only while you are a college student and can be easily missed or overlooked.

I can't tell you how many times adults have said to Tom and me, "I wish I had known about this while I was in college." By reading this book you will know! Many of these success-attracting techniques can be utilized no matter where you are in life's journey, but they are especially applicable for college students.

In this book we share the concepts and actions that these highly successful people utilized so that anyone can follow in their footsteps.

Some of their names will be familiar to you:

- Oprah Winfrey
- Warren Buffett
- Elon Musk
- Wendy Williams
- Carrie Underwood
- Ashton Kutcher
- Missy Franklin
- Justice Thurgood Marshall
- US Presidents
- and many others

You will read about CEOs of Fortune 500 companies, actors, artists and authors. You will read about athletes that went pro and others that didn't, but still found success.

Other people that Tom and I chose to showcase will be new to you. Some of these people we know personally from our years of high school and college advising and others we sought out just to be able to share their stories.

In *College Secrets of Highly Successful People* you will learn powerful secrets that you can use to catapult your own success. It is written especially for those who are in college, or soon to enter college, so that you will not miss out on the opportunities that are unique to the college experience. These secrets, however, have helped many people who have already graduated from college and even those who never intend to enroll. The one common denominator is that these secrets will only work for the person who is intentional about drawing success to their door.

How Do We Define Success?

- Financial and material acquisition
- Changed the world for the better
- Discovered their passion
- Uniquely solved problems
- Found lifelong friendships and connections
- Entered professions that are traditionally difficult to access
- Overcame significant hardships to live a joy-filled life
- Launched their career before they even graduated

Everyone wants success, whether it is to make millions of dollars, to become famous and influential or just to be happy in relationships and life. The difficult thing is figuring out how to get there.

Many people think that going to college will get them the success that they crave, but a college degree alone is not enough. That is like saying if I stay in a garage long enough, I'll become a skilled mechanic. You have to get your hands dirty and be willing to crawl under the cars to really see how things work.

Tom and I have spent many years "getting our hands dirty." We have consulted and advised thousands of high school kids and college students both professionally and personally. We have watched as the trajectory of their lives unfolded. We have seen what has worked for them and what hasn't.

We have researched the college careers and subsequent lives of famous individuals to compare to our own students to see if our hypothesis of best practices was consistent. It has been an unofficial research project that has taken decades to complete.

The most important thing we discovered is this: when it comes to success there is one important element that most people, especially college students, are missing.

- It is the one thing that will allow students to launch their careers even before they graduate
- It is the one thing that will help individuals recognize small opportunities that can be leveraged into life-changing advantages
- It is the element that will help people establish life-long valuable relationships that otherwise might be missed

This most important element that can change any life for the better and draw success to one's door is intentionality.

What Is Intentionality?

I'm going to tell you about an incident from my childhood that will best explain intentionality and how you can use it to make a path for success to find you.

"Lindy!" my mother hollered, "What is that squirrel doing at our door?" I was 10 years old and my family lived in Skokie, a suburb just north of Chicago. There were trees in our neighborhood, but the only wildlife we ever saw were squirrels and rabbits. I loved the squirrels especially because they were so playful. They would chase each other leaping through the tree branches and racing across the tops of the fences. I especially loved their bushy tails that twitched with excitement when they were engaged in activity. I wanted to touch a squirrel.

I knew that squirrels liked peanuts so I set out on a plan to attract the furry critters to me. The squirrels were cautious and wouldn't come into our yard, so I started by placing a small pile of peanuts near the edge of the grass. When I was gone the squirrels sneaked in and consumed them, but I didn't get to see it happen.

The next day I put just a couple of peanuts in the same place as I had before and then added a few more nuts about 8 inches closer to the house. I waited inside at the window, but it wasn't until I tired of watching and moved on to some other endeavor that the nuts again disappeared.

I continued to add the tempting treats each day, creating a path that got ever deeper into our yard. The squirrels were getting bolder and more comfortable getting closer to our human abode. I was able to see the little thieves in action.

I decided it was time to introduce myself to them. I sat on the steps of the house and watched as the squirrels tentatively inched their way close enough to grab a treat and run away. The next day I sat closer to the trail of treats just to show them they needn't be afraid of me.

This was my summer project, my adventure and my science experiment. If my parents had known what I was up to they would have disapproved. They had told me many times that squirrels bite and I was to leave them alone, but my curiosity and desire to touch a squirrel drove me to try to prove them wrong.

Before the summer had ended, I had one little squirrel so addicted to peanuts that she would place her front paws on my outstretched fingers and reach with her mouth all the way to the base of my palm to grab a nut. This allowed me to touch her furry underbelly with my fingertips. My patience had paid off! Success was literally in my hands.

Unfortunately, the squirrel didn't understand when I moved on to other interests and the experiment ended. That was when she came knocking - or should I say clawing - at our door! My parents were not very happy with my Jane Goodall explanation of wanting to be one with nature!

Drawing success to your door is a lot like my adventure with the squirrel. You cannot demand that it come to you as though you are entitled to it. You need to lay out a path that will entice success to come to you. You need to find the things that success feeds upon and use them as bait. But how do you know what you need to do to draw that success to you?

The simple answer is that you must learn from others who have intentionally or serendipitously done it for themselves. Then follow and imitate their path with intention.

That is the purpose of *College Secrets of Highly Successful People*, to tell you the stories of those who have become very successful and what they did in college that set them on the path to their success.

Success Is Not Limited to the Lucky, Privileged or Affluent

Many voices today will tell you that success is limited to the lucky few. In reality, there are more opportunities today for success than there have ever been. Success doesn't come just to the privileged, the affluent or the socially connected. Success does not just happen for the lucky who seem to be in the right place at the right time. In fact, in *College Secrets of Highly Successful People* we reveal the secret of how you can create your own luck!

Success is drawn to those who are diligent and willing to be mentored by others. Success is attracted to people with problem-solving ideas and great ideas come more often to the needy, the ones who are searching for a solution that cannot be bought at any price.

You may have heard the old adage that "necessity is the mother of invention." Anyone stranded in the wilderness can attest to how creative one can be when left without the conveniences of home.

Tom and I have seen students who entered college with nothing but a dream and pushed through to accomplish amazing things. One young woman who is close to our hearts was released by the foster care program when she turned 18 and had no family to turn to and no place to go.

She enlisted in the military, not only to serve her country but also to earn her college tuition through the GI program. She had suffered many unspeakable situations in her life but chose to be a victor rather than a victim. Today, she is a college graduate, a role model and a happily married mom of four.

We have also seen others that had every advantage given to them only to lose it all through poor choices or by following the wrong people. It is entirely within your power to draw success to your door regardless of your background or connections, but you must take the steps necessary to make it happen.

Success is drawn to people who search for it and bait it with acts of intentionality. In *College Secrets of Highly Successful People* you will read about:

- The student who turned down 5 million dollars just to go to college and why she says it was worth it
- The student who came up with a solution to help his classmates and inadvertently launched a multi-million dollar business for himself
- The one thing a student did that earned him a job in a major film studio and that another used to get into the financial industry
- How students found the career and passion of their lives through dealing with devastating personal losses
- The unique way a student managed to get influential people to mentor and advise him right into huge success
- How students found the right people with whom they could build alliances and bring their dreams to reality
- The one course that a student credits for his massive success and that he believes can improve anyone's life.
- And many more

Warning!

Tom and I want to caution you. If you continue to read this book you will discover powerful insider tips that most people do not know. These concepts, if you follow them, whether you go to college or not, can lead to expanding your life and future success in ways you never imagined. If you are okay with that, then we welcome you to Chapter One.

1

Expect Major Changes

"The only way to do great work is to love what you do. If you
haven't found it yet, keep looking. Don't settle. As with all
matters of the heart, you'll know when you find it."
— Steve Jobs

College is a time of change. Students are stepping into
roles that require more personal responsibility than most
of them have ever known before. No one will be telling
them what classes to take or how to best use their time.
They discover they must take care of their daily needs like
laundry and meals, but also figure out how to help
themselves when they become lonely, sick or discouraged.

One of the toughest components of college is that the
students must look into the future and choose a major that
they will focus on for four years to get their degree. The
majority of college students have no idea what they want
to do as an adult.

Tom and I have talked with hundreds of college students who struggled with choosing a major. Some students started with one major and then switched to another, adding to their tuition and time to completion. A major change often added anywhere from one semester to two or more years of study to complete their degree.

Ironically, most college graduates end up working in a totally different area than their major. One college student who couldn't decide between four majors ended up doing them all.

Can't Decide? Do it All

While growing up, DW ran with a fun group of guys. They were reckless and adventurous. There wasn't a lot of adult supervision, so they could take dares and run wild. DW's dad was a preacher for two churches and held another job as well. His mom was a strong, godly woman who ran a beauty shop. They impressed upon their son the principles of making good choices and doing right by other people.

When DW was 14 his parents' strong personalities and differences in upbringing came to a breaking point. They divorced. DW said this hit him hard and he began acting out and rebelling against all rules and authority. His mom felt that without her husband's help she might not be able to raise a teenage son by herself.

There were too many factors in the neighborhood that made her worry for his future, so she enrolled him in Oakland Military Academy. This took him out of the neighborhood and kept him from being drawn into the gangs and incidents of crime to which many of his friends fell prey.

OMA was a private prep school in New Windsor, N.Y. and DW's life flourished there. He made new friends, played in the band and became a basketball star. He enjoyed this high school and began to dream about his own future and what it would hold for him.

After graduation he set his sights on pursuing the pre-med program at Fordham University in the Bronx. He tried out for the basketball team there as a walk-on and out of the 80 other guys competing, he earned a defensive spot on the team. Although he never started for the team, he stuck with it for two years.

When he didn't do well in some of the science courses, he decided that pre-med was not for him after all. He considered changing to a political science major, but that did not hold his interest for long either. DW decided to pursue a journalism major, but this field did not generate the kind of passion that he wanted.

At age 20 and with no final goal in mind, he took a semester off to rethink the direction for his life. He had enjoyed being a part of the Boys and Girls Club of America since he was 6 years old, so he decided to work for Camp Sloane YMCA as the Creative Arts Director to help other kids.

He loved working with the kids and teaching them to rise above their personal life circumstances. At the end of the camp the counselors pulled together a drama presentation for the kids. DW memorized his lines and spent a lot of time contemplating the demeanor that his character should demonstrate. When the evening of the show came around DW captivated the audience.

After the applause both the kids and the other camp leaders rushed him to tell him what a great job he had done. That was the moment when he knew what he would do with his life. He would become an actor. He returned to college and changed his paperwork to reflect his choice of theater major.

DW, whose full name is Denzel Washington, did not study pre-med, but he has spent many years playing a doctor on *St. Elsewhere*. He never became a journalist, but he played one in *The Pelican Brief*. He has portrayed a coach, a politician, a soldier and a gangster.

Because of his deep Christian faith, he has pondered the thought that perhaps he should have been a preacher. However, he said that he is aware that because of the massive amount of acting work he has done and by winning two Oscars he has become a role model and he does not take that responsibility lightly.

Denzel and his wife have dedicated themselves to keeping their marriage strong for over 35 years. That is quite a feat for a Hollywood couple! He also uses his wealth to support the things he believes in like giving to his church, his alma mater and the Boys and Girls Club of America. He has shown that no matter what he chose for his major he could still do it all.

Major Decisions

Sean came to me in a panic. He had no idea of what his major should be, and he had to commit to one before he could register for his junior year of classes. As his college advisor I directed him to various websites where he learned more about different career tracks, what the salaries would be and if the industry was growing or shrinking. With economic changes in the country I told him he needed to pursue a major that would lead to a job that would still be around in two years.

Even more important than knowing about the job or career, however, I told Sean he needed to know if he would be happy in a particular career. "That is like trying to tell the future, and who does that?" Sean replied.

I assured him that choosing a major does not chisel it in stone. He would be able to change majors if later he felt that he had made a big mistake. In fact, 50% of college students change their majors at least once during their four years of studies. Choosing one's major is a scary commitment, especially when you haven't decided on a career.

I told him about a few famous people he might know that got their degree in one thing but ended up being highly successful in a totally different field. I assured him that this is very common.

There are careers that are changing and disappearing faster than ever before in the history of the world. With the advent of ever more sophisticated computers it is predicted that some nursing positions and entry level law positions will be lost to question-answering computer systems like IBM's Watson.

Watson can diagnose medical situations faster than a human nurse. It will have a substantial impact on the medical industry. Likewise, many commonly asked legal questions can be answered by computers as well. It is important to stay on top of where each industry is headed.

Through a series of exercises from our online training program *College Superhero Secrets,* I was able to help Sean identify what he enjoyed doing and what he was good at. It helped him to think back to his childhood days and remember his favorite pastimes. He was then able to research and match those skills to various career opportunities.

Oprah Winfrey and Ray Romano

Having a college degree opens many doors of opportunity, but those doors may end up taking you in a direction you never imagined. Oprah Winfrey, the very successful talk show host and author began her career as the first black woman to anchor a local TV news program.

You would think that she would have majored in journalism. However, her major was speech communications and drama. That major ended up working very well for her because she was able to find the drama and entertainment value in every guest she had on her show. She has also acted in several movies.

As a comedian and actor, Ray Romano has brought laughter to millions. His TV sitcom *Everybody Loves Raymond* won him an Emmy award. His voice caused us to fall in love with Manny the woolly mammoth in the *Ice Age* films. Surprisingly he did not major in drama or theater. He went to Queens College to become an accountant! I doubt he would have generated much laughter doing audits!

U. S. Chief Justice Thurgood Marshall

Even U.S. Chief Justice Thurgood Marshall, who became the first African-American to serve on the Supreme Court of the United States started his undergrad studies with a plan to be a dentist. That is a huge change of direction! When asked about why he chose to get into law, he said, "I don't know. The nearest I can get is that my dad, my brother and I had the most violent arguments you ever heard about anything. I guess we argued five out of seven nights at the dinner table."

Interesting to note is that one of the things his father often enjoyed doing was to sit in the courthouse to hear the cases being tried. He would then come home and retell his sons the stories and the arguments he had heard.

Jeremy, another student, was an avid baseball card collector. He was first given some baseball cards when he was a little kid. They fascinated him. He saved his money to invest in more of them. He often sorted his cards and counted and stacked them. He bought magazines where he could look up the value of his cards and tracked how much certain cards were increasing or dropping in value.

This student recognized his intrigue with numbers and market data and analysis. Not surprisingly, he chose to major in business and now works with numbers all day long at a large financial firm. Those are the types of things to look for when trying to determine a major.

Deanna chose English literature as her major because she loved to read. However, as she continued through her program, she began to worry that she might have a difficult time connecting her degree to a career. When I urged her to type in her choice of major on the website MyMajors.com, the career list that was generated was very short. The only career listed was that she could become a professor of the same English literature courses.

She decided to expand her future job possibilities by also earning her teaching certificate. When she graduated, she found a position as the reading specialist at a grade school. It was the perfect combination for her, working with children and books.

Another young woman was frustrated because she wanted to get a degree in biology. Her parents felt that her talent and intellectual leanings would be better served by majoring in engineering. She told me she found a compromise that would satisfy both her desire and that of her parents. She grinned when she revealed that she was pursuing bio-engineering.

The Physical Therapist

Tal Blair is a very gifted physical therapist (PT). I assumed that he had chosen that field because he or someone he knew must have had an injury that required the services of a PT in the past, but that was not the case. When I asked him how he got into the field his answer surprised me.

Tal was convinced he wanted to be an architect. He was creative and enjoyed drawing and inventing things. However, once he was in college and got deeper into his courses, he found that even though he liked to draw and was very good at it, the discipline of architecture did not hold his interest. He struggled with a focus and admitted that he changed his major more than a few times trying to find a suitable career path.

He talked to friends and family about what they thought he should do. He got opinions from people who hated their jobs and opinions from people who thought their own careers were the best, but nothing they described seemed to be the right fit for Tal. His mom suggested that he talk with one of her friends who was a PT and loved her profession. At the time Tal admits he didn't even know what a PT did.

He followed through on his mom's suggestion and had a conversation with the physical therapist. The PT had Tal shadow her during a typical day. She sat with each of her patients listening to them describe their struggles with joint and muscle stiffness or pain. She then prescribed specific movements that over time would alleviate the pain. Finally, she assisted each patient to complete various stretches and exercises that increased their mobility.

The job of the PT required creativity to determine the needs and solutions for each patient. He could see himself doing this kind of work and decided to pursue that career. He was warned that to be a physical therapist he would be required to first get a bachelor's degree, then a master's degree and finally his doctorate. It would be a long journey.

The program required that he study human physiology and biology, so he decided to get an education degree with an emphasis in exercise science. His reasoning was that by the time he completed his undergrad program, if he no longer wanted to continue the additional education to become a PT, he could instead teach at the high school level.

The pre-med courses fascinated him, and he completed the long years of study that he needed to become a physical therapist. Ironically, even though he left the architecture program Tal, like an architect, used his creativity in the hours after his clinic closed each day designing, developing and inventing an ingenious tool called the Motion Guidance System.

This tool is used to help patients monitor the accuracy of their own movements during therapy so that they regain their mobility and strength faster. PTs throughout the world today are utilizing his MG System in their practices.

Choosing a college major can feel like trying to select a book from the Library of Congress without access to the e-catalog. Often a college advisor will ask the student, "What classes do you enjoy? Pick a major that requires more courses like that."

Unfortunately, that advice is not enough. Getting the degree is not the end of the student's journey; it is the beginning. Many students will choose a major in women's studies or environmental studies because they like the classes. I always advise them that any major that ends in the word "studies" tends to limit the graduate to only one career door, a profession teaching those same courses. Highly successful people choose to give themselves more career options than a single path.

BONUS: The First 30 Days
In College Essential Checklist

College is an exciting time of life, but it also can be difficult to navigate through all the decisions and responsibilities it requires.

Set yourself up for success by downloading this FREE checklist of the most important things you must do when you arrive on campus.

Go to:

www.AmericasCollegeAdvisors.com/First30

2

Your Career Starts in College

"There are many things in life that will catch your eye, but only a few will catch your heart. Do those."
— Michael Nolan

From the first day that our oldest son Jeremy set foot on campus at Grand Canyon University he knew he wanted to take advantage of the work study option offered through the FAFSA, Free Application for Student Aid program. He made this a priority and before he signed any papers or picked out his classes, he mentioned his desire to the business office.

The woman who was working with him on getting enrolled was impressed with his pleasant demeanor and she jumped at the chance to hire him. She said, "Don't say anything about this to your student advisor, because we want you in our office!" She thrust a job application in front of him and he was off and running.

On Campus Jobs

There are a limited number of work study jobs available at a college and because Jeremy asked about his opportunities immediately, he got a prize one. His job consisted of computing and handing out the pay checks to all the campus employees on an ongoing basis. Everyone who came to see him was in a great mood because they were coming to pick up a check. Also, because it was a work study job his hours were scheduled around his classes. Jeremy was even excused to participate in the baseball practices since he was on the team. A job off campus would not be so accommodating.

Jeremy enjoyed his job and worked at the business office all four years of his college, building friendships, earning money and growing his responsibilities. By the time he was ready to toss his cap into the air he had not only earned a degree in business administration but had also earned the title of Business Office Manager, with four years of experience.

When he added that to his resume and spoke with a recruiter for Vanguard Financial Group he was hired! Many of his friends had the dilemma of earning their degree, but no work experience. It took them several months post-graduation to land an entry level position anywhere. Jeremy was able to walk right into the industry of his choosing because of the work study program.

Our youngest son Ryan also accepted a job through work study, but he chose to work in the computer lab on campus. His title was IT or Technical Support. The job consisted of answering phone calls from students who were unable to access online courses or were having other troubles with their technology and he would walk them through the steps to fix the problem.

Before he took the job, Ryan explained that he didn't know that much about computers and was concerned that he may not know the answers that were required. The manager at the lab handed him a manual and said, "What you don't know you can look up in this book. Just walk the student through the trouble-shooting questions and you will find the answers."

Most of the calls that Ryan got described a problem that he was easily able to resolve, such as having the students adjust the setting to allow cookies on their computer so that the required applications would pop up. Between calls he was able to work on his own course assignments. He was getting paid to do homework and getting valuable experience in technology at the same time!

Ryan also took the position of Assistant Intramural Director. This job had him scheduling and coaching intramural teams on campus. Sometimes when there weren't enough players to show up to a game he even got to play as a substitute. That job paid him while he was doing something he loved! It was a win-win.

Although the work study jobs are flexible to work around a student's schedule, it is critical to treat them as a job. Being too casual, showing up late or not at all will destroy any advantage they may give you. It is an opportunity to practice professionalism and to prove yourself to your employer.

The on-campus job opportunities are varied and get filled very quickly. It is important to talk to the advisor even before you arrive on campus and ask what is available.

Those who ask first have the pick of the jobs. It prevents the student from falling into the group of unemployed graduates who say, "I have my degree but can't get a job because two to three years of experience is required as well."

Off Campus Jobs

There are other ways to get experience and connections and that is by taking advantage of internships. These can be paid or unpaid and are offered through businesses who are looking to hire college students on a temporary basis.

Internships are amazing opportunities that allow you to see behind the curtain of industries that may be especially difficult to break into. They allow you to meet people who are already in the industry. If you do a good job in your internship, the people you worked for and alongside may be willing to write you a letter of recommendation which is worth gold to you!

Not every internship will result in a job offer, but all of them will give you insights into what you want to do or not want to do in the future. We will be discussing internships in greater detail in a later chapter where you will discover how a famous film director walked right into his career by way of an internship.

Daniel Fazzina wanted to break into TV or radio and knew that his best bet would be to take advantage of every internship he could find. His college, St. John's University in New York, put a high emphasis on internships and he ended up doing five different ones before he graduated!

He worked behind the camera at major events and on the set at TV stations. He loved it all but wasn't sure where the best fit would be for him.

His favorite event was a short-term internship where he was assigned to run the technology for the Urbana Conference. This is InterVarsity's Student Missions Conference. The five-day event is held annually in large venues in the United States or Canada during the winter break between December and the start of the January semester. Sixteen thousand college students, faculty, recent graduates, pastors and missionary organizations converge to discover mission opportunities and to engage in worship sessions, seminars and Bible studies.

Daniel said the energy was electric. He got a glimpse of how he could do something that was personally meaningful with his skills. Although he had worked in the newsrooms of national TV stations, this event was the one that directed the future of his life.

Today Daniel is the host and producer of Divine Intervention Radio where he interviews people who have experienced the hand of God in miraculous ways. He loves the work he does and feels that the internship he did with Urbana was instrumental in pointing him in the direction that he was to go.

Create Your Own Opportunities

Some colleges do not have the connections that a student needs to get into an internship. The Secret Millionaire, James Malinchak, found himself in that exact situation when he was a college student just starting out. It seemed like he would be stuck with limited opportunities and he had big plans for his life.

When Tom and I met with James he told us he grew up in a poor steel town in Pennsylvania in a blue-collar family. If he had not received a basketball scholarship, he would not have been able to go to college at all. The money was just not there for him.

He was picked up to play for the University of Cincinnati, transferred to the University of Pennsylvania at Johnstown and finally ended up at the University of Hawaii in Hilo. His plan was always to play for the NBA, but when an injury blew out his knee that plan was over. Even the surgery that followed could not restore him to the level of basketball prowess he once had.

James had always had a Plan B since he was aware that athletic dreams are often snuffed out. He was disappointed but threw himself into his business major and worked to become a star in that field like he had been on the basketball court. He knew that an internship would give him an edge when it came time to apply for jobs so he set out to find one with a major financial company. He talked to the career center on campus and was informed that his school did not have the connections to offer any.

James is not one to take no for an answer. He took his resume and began calling different top companies asking for an appointment to speak with different CEOs and VPs. All he wanted was an internship, but the answer time and again was, "Our company does not offer college internships."

James did not give up. At each interview he presented himself as though he were already working in the industry. He dressed for success in a suit and tie. He conducted himself as a professional. He asked questions about the company and asked for advice on how to best climb the ranks in the financial industry. He asked for referrals of other people to talk to that might be able to help him.

Each time he called to set up another appointment he would mention the name of the person referring him and tell them that this mutual acquaintance had recommended that they meet and speak.

Finally, his persistence paid off. He met with the Vice President and Office Manager of Merrill Lynch who was so impressed with James' professionalism that he made him an offer. The man began by telling James the same thing that he had been told time and again, that the company did not offer internships. "However," he continued, "I will pay you out of my own pocket to have you work for me through the summer."

That was the break James needed. He had a top financial company on his resume, and he had a top official in the company to give him a personal recommendation. The following summer he repeated those steps and landed another internship at a different firm, only this time it was easier for him to get a yes.

Upon graduation James moved to Los Angeles with his business degree in hand and landed a job as a stockbroker with a Wall Street investment firm. Using all the skills he had learned through his dogged quest to land his internships he quickly advanced in his career and became a partner while still in his 20s. He began training others in the company so that they could have the kind of success he had accomplished. He won many national awards and spoke at several conferences.

He discovered that he greatly enjoyed speaking and he was good at it, although he had no intention of making it his profession. But something happened that changed everything.

"I did a lecture at a college," James said, "when a student came up to me afterward and said he really didn't want to come, but his professor made him. Then he said he was so glad he did because what he had heard changed his life."

The idea that he could impact thousands of people's lives through sharing his knowledge on stage gave James a new passion. Today James earns between $20,000 to $100,000 per speaking gig and teaches others the business of successful public speaking through his Big Money Speaker Boot Camps.

You may have even seen him in an episode of ABC TV's *The Secret Millionaire* that ran in 2011. On the show he was placed in an impoverished area for one week with only $44.66 to live on. He volunteered at various non-profits and got to know the people who were making a difference in their community but no one knew exactly who he was or why he was there.

At the close of the week he surprised the people he got to know with checks of multiple thousands of dollars to help them continue their work. The money for those checks came from his own bank account.

Whether you plan to pursue an internship off campus like Daniel and James or a work study job on campus like Jeremy and Ryan, the key to it being a career launch is to approach it with professionalism. Every opportunity can be advantageous to your life, but only if you treat it as the valuable opportunity that it is.

3

Billionaire Dropouts

"Always, always have a plan."
— Rick Riordan, NY Times bestselling author

It wasn't a bad question or even a hard question that the woman in the TV audience asked, but it made the host Wendy Williams burst into tears. She took out her tissues and blotted the moisture from her face as she pondered the question.

The woman told Wendy that she had a son who had just started his freshman year of college, but he had already decided that college was not for him. Her question was, should she let him drop out or make him continue in college. Wendy's immediate eruption in tears brought confusion and silence to the audience. What was going on?

Wendy explained that her son Kevin Hunter, Jr. was also a freshman in college and they were going through the same thing with him. Wendy took a deep breath and said, "College is not for everyone. Period. But what you have to have in the Hunter household and now in yours," she said pointing her finger at the mom, "you have to have a plan. And it has to be a solid plan!" Wendy went on to say that if the mom forced him to continue, he would just flunk out and waste their money.

Her advice was exactly right. Dropping out of college is not a plan for success. However, many people insist that Mark Zuckerberg and the other billionaire dropouts proved that they didn't need college to be successful.

I took a long look into what exactly these famous dropouts did during their collegiate year(s) and I discovered that college did indeed help to catapult them into success, although not by way of a degree. The people they met and the ideas that were generated on campus were necessary foundations to the wealth that they built after leaving their respective colleges.

Bill Gates

The founder of Microsoft is the most famous of college dropouts. He left college not only because he was not challenged at Harvard, but also because he had a business idea that would demand all of his attention. Within two years of enrollment he had easily completed the most advanced math courses and graduate level computer science courses that the college had to offer. His desire was to create software for computers and there seemed to be nothing more that the college could teach him that he hadn't already learned on his own. That is not usually the case for most dropouts.

Gates was born in 1955 and was drawn to technology. He learned about computers as they were being developed, long before most Americans could imagine ever having one in their homes. The moms group that raised funds for his junior high school held a rummage sale. From the proceeds they bought an early pre-home computer model that used data punch cards to store information. With it was a block of computer time for the school's students to use. Gates was first in line to use it and found a way to override the system so that he could get even more time on it. He was given time out of his math classes to work with the computer. Here is where he immersed himself in learning to talk to machines.

Like most 13-year-old kids Gates wanted to earn some money. He and his childhood friend Paul Allen did not set up a lemonade stand or deliver newspapers. Instead they created a computer program that had commercial value. They developed Trac-O-Data, a program that counted and tracked automobile traffic. The city of Seattle saw the value of it and bought it. That was just the start of his entrepreneurial pursuits.

By 20 years of age Bill Gates had been in college for two years. He was able to use the computers at the college extensively to develop his ideas. He was inspired when he saw the January 1975 issue of *Popular Electronics* that featured the Altair 8800, a microcomputer designed by MITS for individuals to use at home. The company offered a kit that contained all the components and instructions needed for an individual to build their own working computer. MITS expected only hobbyists to be interested in it. What they underestimated was the national reaction. They were inundated with thousands of sales for the world's first home computer.

This triggered an explosive reaction in Gates's mind. He realized that if people wanted home computers, they would also need software to be able to utilize it and that is what he was driven to design. Seated on his dorm room bed he dialed the office of MITS and offered to write computer language for them.

It took some convincing, but eventually the computer language he developed called BASIC was purchased by MITS for $3,000 plus royalties.

Across the hall in the same dorm was his classmate Steve Ballmer. Besides access to computers, Ballmer was the second-best thing Gates got out of college. He was concerned that Gates was always studying or working on projects. College was supposed to be a time for having fun and Ballmer nagged Gates to join in on some of the events and social clubs on campus. If it weren't for Ballmer, Gates might never have done anything besides study. The two became good friends.

Gates never did create a plan that would lead to a degree at Harvard, but he did spend a lot of time on their computers. He decided it was time for him to start his own computer software business.

He took a leave of absence from college and with a call to his childhood friend, Paul Allen, headed to Albuquerque, New Mexico to start his company, Microsoft. Paul Allen joined him there. Ballmer was sorry to see Gates go but stayed the course to graduate with honors. He later joined Microsoft as one of its earliest employees. Their friendship endured and when Gates stepped down as CEO of the company, Ballmer took his place.

Gates said, "if things [Microsoft] hadn't worked out, I could always go back to school. I was officially on leave."

Mark Zuckerberg

Mark Zuckerberg grew up in the 80's and 90's using computers from the time he could walk. His parents recognized Zuckerberg's fascination with computers and taught him how to do BASIC programming. When he was no longer challenged by that his father, who owned a dental practice, hired a software developer to tutor him.

To show his dad that the tutoring was valuable and appreciated, Mark created a program that would connect the computers at home with the ones at his father's dental office so that they could share information with one another. This was very cutting edge at the time. It was his first practical creation using his computer knowledge.

By the time he was in high school he had been recognized by PC Magazine for a music program he built that would learn the listener's music preferences, a predecessor of Pandora. Some called him a programming prodigy.

He enrolled at Harvard studying psychology and computer science, but it was the social aspect of college that really motivated him. He joined a fraternity and wrote a program called CourseMatch that students could use to choose classes and set their schedules to coincide with the classes that their friends had signed up to attend.

He built another site called Facemash that was meant to be a game. Using technology, he ripped the photos of students from the Harvard catalogs of dorm residents and paired similar faces side by side. On the site students were instructed to vote which student was better looking. The ratings were "hot" or "not" and Zuckerberg's program tabulated rankings for each student.

Although highly popular, it caused an outcry from many students that it was completely inappropriate and offensive. Facemash was shut down within three days and Zuckerberg was required to apologize to the entire student body.

Rather than being halted in his pursuits, Zuckerberg was actually buoyed by the experience to produce something equally as popular, but without the negative repercussions. He had also gained a reputation on campus as being a programing genius, so others began to gravitate to him.

Zuckerberg was approached by three students who had an idea and asked him to create it for them. They divulged their secret ideas to him and told him they would pay him for his expertise. The program would be a social networking site for the school called the Harvard Connection. The students envisioned it to be similar to a dating site.

Zuckerberg listened to their ideas and became inspired. His concept was to take their idea but expand it beyond the students at Harvard. He saw their concept as a flower in a pot. He wanted to make a garden that covered the whole world. Instead of completing their project, he built a similar site of his own calling it "The Facebook" and launched it first.

The project became his passion. He dropped out of college to work on developing this program into Facebook as we know it now.

The three students who first approached him with the initial idea filed a lawsuit against Zuckerberg and received a hefty settlement in Facebook shares, but the little idea that was birthed from a dorm room discussion had grown into a behemoth business.

College did indeed enrich Zuckerberg's life and career. In fact, it could be argued that if he had not gone to college Facebook might never have been born.

One more point of value for his time at Harvard: Zuckerberg met his wife and business partner Priscilla Chan at a fraternity party he was attending there. They married several years later.

Brian Scudamore

Brian left college for junk. His father was a respected liver transplant surgeon and wanted to see his son excel in an equally respectable career. Although he was wealthy, he insisted that Brian make his own way as an adult, not relying on family money to get him by. His dad knew that character would get him further in life than comfort and character is often developed through hardship.

Brian didn't like that philosophy very much at the time, but the very stress that his college bills and living expenses put on him was the catalyst that stoked the fire of his business. He said that earning money was constantly on his mind. He pursued a degree in business and worked at various jobs to pay his way through college.

One day when he was in a McDonald's restaurant, he saw a pickup truck as it rolled through the drive through lane. It was filled with junk. Now, Brian is a bit of a neat freak. He dislikes clutter and even as a child he kept his room clear of stuff. When he was four years old, he drew a picture for his grandmother of himself sweeping stuff out of the street. He did not pick through other's stuff or wish he had more stuff. He basically didn't like stuff.

However, this day the truck filled with junk held his attention. "I should haul junk!" he thought. He took $700 and bought a beat-up truck and within one week he had a business helping other people get rid of their excess junk. He was 18 years old, studying business and running a business.

By age 23 he had not yet completed his degree, but he did have a viable business. Much to the disappointment of his dad he dropped out of college to give his company his full attention. To continue his education so that he would make wise choices for his business he sought out other entrepreneurs and asked for their advice.

Five years later he had a junk hauling business worth one million dollars, but he was discouraged. He saw reports in the newspaper about his techie peers building multiple million-dollar businesses. He began to question if he had done the right thing.

Brian began imagining where he would like to be five years further down the road. He wrote out dream goals that seemed unreachable and set a deadline to attain them. He wanted to franchise his company to be in 30 cities. He added to his list that he wanted to have shiny new trucks and drivers who had good people skills. He wanted to be so successful that he would be invited onto the Oprah Winfrey show. He didn't know how it would happen, but once it was on his list it became a priority to pursue.

With this perspective, and guided by his list, he fired his entire staff to find new employees that shared his vision, not just people who wanted to earn a paycheck. He renamed his company 1-800-GOT-JUNK? which was a significant boost to his brand, but there was a problem. The phone number he wanted for his business was owned by the Idaho Department of Transportation. He had to persistently beg the IDT to give him the use of that number. Eventually they relented and gave him the number without any payment required.

Within one year of making his list he had reached his goals. He had even hugged Oprah Winfrey in the green room of her show when his company was featured for a segment she was doing on hoarding.

Brian insists that his employees maintain a list of 101 dream goals. He believes in dreams no matter how audacious. He has seen many of these imaginings come true. He has started several additional companies and built an empire that is worth hundreds of millions of dollars. I am sure becoming a billionaire dropout is on his list.

John Mackey

The Whole Foods grocery store empire was cooked up on the campus of Texas University in Austin. Being a philosophy and religion major, John Mackey wasn't looking to start a business - he was looking to start a relationship. He needed some new places to seek out a girlfriend and thought that the university vegetarian co-op dorm just might be his meal ticket.

He joined up and moved in and was pleased to discover that it was a very popular place for women to be. He smiled, started up casual conversations and hoped no one could smell the burger on his breath. However, when he met Renee Lawson Hardy at the co-op, he gave up meat for good. The two began spending a lot of time together between classes.

Renee often complained that when they were off campus there was nothing in Austin, Texas that catered to vegetarians. In fact, there was nothing like what they wanted in all of Texas, a state that prides itself on its beef production. The more the two discussed this dilemma the more they fixated on a plan to remedy the situation.

Mackey dropped out of college and took on the role of buyer for the co-op. He was learning a lot about how fresh foods were acquired and he became fascinated by the idea of healthier eating.

Mackey and Lawson Hardy decided to go out on their own and give this business a try. They borrowed $10,000 and contacted the local farmers about what it would take to have them bring their fresh produce to their store daily. They rented an old house where they could use the bottom two floors for their grocery store and health food restaurant. There was just enough room on the third floor for a bed, so that is where Mackey and Lawson Hardy slept.

The vegetarian store and restaurant struggled for two years, but the customers they won over were fiercely loyal. Mackey wanted to expand so he talked with another local natural food store and negotiated a merger. When that deal went through the four owners changed the name to Whole Foods Market. With this new venue they decided to add meat, beer and wine to their offerings.

The Austin hippy community and university crowd spread the word and it became an overnight success. They were not without their challenges, however.

This company in its new location was nearly wiped out by a massive flood for which they had no flood insurance. However, the community and loyal fans rallied around them. Volunteers came forward to help them clean up the mess. The banks extended credit lines and investors became more generous. Even their employees put in extra hours for no pay to get the store back open.

Whole Foods began as a hippy hang-out in a university town but has since grown exponentially as the nation's interest in healthy eating has exploded into all demographics. It is now an empire worth multiple billions of dollars.

John Mackey's interest in philosophy and religion has grown, too. He is a staunch believer in capitalism as he has seen his own idea grow into a business that has provided jobs for thousands of families.

He has also been able to make life better for others through his charitable giving. The year he turned 53 he announced to his employees and company board that he was reducing his salary to $1. He was choosing to work "simply for the joy of work itself." His future stock options were all donated to the company's charitable giving foundations.

John said he spent nearly six years in college taking various courses that interested him. He saw himself as a generalist, not pursuing a degree but pursuing knowledge. He chose courses in a variety of different specialties and those courses are the main reason he has been successful in his business.

Steve Jobs and Aquaman (Jason Momoa)

College is a unique environment where young people converge from all over the world to increase their education and discover new ideas. When used correctly college can be like joining a mastermind or creativity lab. Students can link up with individuals who have similar goals or interests and brainstorm together on innovative ideas. There is also the opportunity to find people who have strengths different than their own. Working together on one idea is like a having many different spokes to attach to the hub of a wheel. Outside of college it is harder to find those folks who can become the spokes.

Sometimes, however, it is just one course that changes a student's perspective. Although Steve Jobs was officially enrolled at Reed College for only six months, he stayed nearby and audited classes that interested him. The cost of tuition was a key factor in his decision to drop out of a degree program. He also did not want his parents to carry the burden of tuition.

When he spoke at Stanford University about his time in college, he credited one class in particular for making his model of the Mac computer better than it would ever have been. Jobs said, "If I had never dropped in on that single calligraphy course in college, the Mac would have never had multiple typefaces or proportionally spaced fonts." He was very grateful for what he learned in that course even though at the time he did not know how he would use the knowledge he gained.

Another student, Jason Momoa, who did not stick with his college plans for very long always gets a chuckle when he explains that his first declared major was marine biology. Whatever courses he completed in that major before he left to join the cast of *Bay Watch* just may have set him up to be able to talk to fish in his blockbuster movie *Aquaman*!

4

Transform Your Life: Make Your Own Luck

"One is sure to fail one time or another, but success requires
lots of endeavor and good luck."
— Steven Spielberg

Have you ever known someone that just seemed to have
everything good happen to him or her? If they interview
for an internship or job, they get it. If they audition for a
part, they get it. They seem to meet the right people and
be at the right place at the right time to get opportunities
or rewards that you wish were yours. It can be very
annoying.

You may feel like others always get the breaks. Well, what
if I told you how you can create your own luck so that you
could have good things befall you too? Would you be
interested? Whether speaking to college students or their
parents, I have never had anyone say no to this
proposition.

Tom and I had the opportunity to meet and talk with movie and TV actor Glenn Morshower. He has this super-power of creating his own "luck" and told us about how he used it to insure movie roles for the rest of his life!

You may not recognize his name, but you would probably recognize his face or voice from the many roles he has played. He is the actor most known as "Oh, that guy!" Among his best-known roles was as Aaron Pierce, Secret Service Agent to the President of the United States in the original TV series *24*. He has also appeared in *The Resident,* the *Transformers* movies and is one of the Commanders on the videogame *Call of Duty: Modern Warfare II*.

He told us about a time in his career when he was hired by award winning director Michael Bay to play a significant role in the movie *Pearl Harbor*. Since the movie shoot would be taking place in another state, he cleared his schedule, booked a flight and a hotel and arrived on set ready to start at his specific call time.

When he checked in with the producer, he was told that he did not have a part in the movie. Someone else was booked for the role that he thought he had. Morshower gave the producer his call sheet that clearly showed his name next to the role in question and then took a step back to let the producer and director work out the logistics of having booked two actors for only one role.

It was a terrible mistake that was going to cost one actor a lot of money and inconvenience for having flown to the movie set only to have to fly home again. It could have created a great deal of embarrassment for the producer and director, especially if the actor made a big deal about the mistake. After all, there were other acting jobs that the actor had to turn down to be on the set for this job. It would be understandable for him to be angry!

Morshower did not put up a fight to be the one chosen for this role. Instead, he chose to have a patient attitude and just wait to hear what they decided. Eventually the director came to him and apologized for the double booking. He needed to give the role to the other actor and asked Morshower, since he was already on set, if he would be willing to take a 30 second non-speaking role instead. Morshower agreed, and his only part in *Pearl Harbor* is that of the man holding flags and waving down a plane. He likes to say he was the best paid extra in that film.

Was he the lucky one? No, the actor who got to play the speaking role was the lucky one in this case. When I explain what happened next, however, you'll realize how Morshower made his own luck. The director, Michael Bay, was so impressed with how graciously and professionally Morshower handled a potentially disastrous mistake that he told him, "Glenn, you will be in every movie I make!"

Michael Bay was true to his word. He cast Morshower in his next movie, *Transformers 2: Revenge of the Fallen*. When he called Glenn Morshower to recruit him to act in the second *Transformers* movie, Morshower said as a way of reminder, "Does it bother you that I was killed in *Transformers One*?" The director replied, "Not in the least!" and cast him again with a new name, "General Morshower."

As an additional bonus, in 2011 Universal Studios opened a new feature, *Transformers 3D: The Ride*. When you board the ride, you will be instructed on what to expect by General Morshower. The actor speaking is Glenn Morshower. He was given a contract stating that he will be paid monthly residuals for the park to use his image for the next 20 years! Pretty lucky guy!

Now Glenn Morshower did not attend college. He pursued acting right out of high school, but the idea of transforming one's circumstances for the better can be used both in college and out. We tell the students in our *College Superhero Secrets* program that a key to creating your own luck is to practice professionalism, just as Morshower did, in everything you do.

Memorable Students

While I was an advisor at an international university there were students whose names everyone knew, and not because they were exceptional students. One student I'll call Carl often called in to the office, rudely demanding to have his latest problem fixed. His name became synonymous with difficult. It was almost as though his attitude was the word "trouble" tattooed on his face that you could even see while on the phone with him. People were reluctant to go the extra mile to get this person the help he needed.

Whenever Carl called, the receptionist would announce the incoming call with his name and no one in the office wanted to take his call. I always volunteered to talk with him because I knew how to calm him down and get him to listen to reason.

On one occasion he was especially agitated. I listened to his rants until he got all of his anger out. He wanted his professor to be fired! He felt that his professor was giving him poor grades just because she didn't like him. He was at risk of not passing the course.

I asked him questions about his interaction with the professor in class. It had not been good. I asked him if he had talked to the professor to find out why his essays were not satisfying the grade requirements. He said he had but he disagreed with her demands.

I reminded him that the professor had the ultimate power in her course. There was no wiggle room there. Either he did it her way or accepted her evaluation without complaint, even if that turned out to be a failing grade.

We hashed it all out and talked it all through. It became obvious that he had not been conducting himself as a professional, but rather as a student who believed he was entitled to more than what he had earned. The professor was just as irritated by his attitude as the advisors in the office had been and was not willing to work with him any longer.

To be fair, this particular professor was tougher than most. By her reputation I knew she did not award an A unless a paper was truly exceptional. I acted as the mediator between Carl and the professor. He needed to make some humble apologies and put in the effort to rewrite several papers according to the guidelines that she required. The professor finally agreed to give him one more chance.

By the end of the semester Carl had pulled up his grade in that course to a B. He told me he had learned a big lesson on the value of being respectful. In fact, he even wrote an email to the professor (that he shared with me) thanking her for working with him. He told her that he learned more in that class than he had in any of his other classes.

On another occasion a frustrated student named Jordan called in to talk about a difficult situation that was beyond his control. He asked his advisor to reach out to his professor whom he believed was being unreasonable. He needed help to remedy the situation.

Jordan was respectful, gracious and polite. Everyone in the office was inspired to do whatever they could to help. He got a solution much more quickly than did Carl. By his attitude alone he had created his own "luck."

The college campus is a microcosm, or miniature city. The students will cross paths with many of the same people throughout their years there. Each student will have many different professors and those professors talk to one another. They extoll the virtues of the wonderfully memorable students and complain about the difficult ones. They remember students' names.

Whether you are aware of it or not, you are building a reputation and word gets around. As one student told me after graduation, "I tell my friends that college is a four-year job interview!" Those professors remember how each student treated them and are the very ones who can provide letters of recommendation or referrals for jobs. You should treat everyone as the valuable assets that they are. It's a great way to create your own "luck."

Most Effective When Least Expected

I personally experienced this amazing phenomenon of being able to transform a tough situation into an amazing one without even realizing what I had done. I had just moved from Arizona to Colorado to start a new job. I would oversee a division that the college had just created, and I was excited about the opportunity. Tom and I were delighted to be in Colorado near family and we began the process of purchasing a home. It looked like everything was moving along just as we had planned.

The college was decorated for the Christmas holidays and I was in a festive mood as I stomped the snow off my boots, stepped into the elevator and punched the button I needed. I was humming a Christmas carol when I stepped onto my floor. I greeted my peers with a smile and "good morning," but no one said anything in return. LeeAnn, my friend and co-worker, pulled me aside and whispered, "They are doing massive layoffs!" I got that punch-in-the-gut feeling and hurried to my desk.

LeeAnn was sure I would be fine because this new division was just created and they needed me there to run it. I had only been at the college for two months, however, so I feared the worst. Sure enough, I got the tap on my shoulder to follow my manager to his office.

"Close the door and sit down," I was told. Both my manager and the Vice President of the college were there and they explained in detail what was happening. I was given papers to sign and procedures to follow. I could hardly focus on what they were saying. My mind was whirling with thoughts. How will I tell my husband? Will we still be able to buy a house? Where will I start looking for a new job?

Then I noticed that the men giving me this dreadful news looked weary and dejected. I realized that they were the same two men who had chosen to hire me. This might be my last chance to thank them. So, I did. I told them how much I had enjoyed this job and thanked them for hiring me in the first place.

They were stunned. All morning they had fielded questions and curses, tears and anger from the many employees that were given their pink slips. My manager said, "Of all the things I expected to hear this morning, thank you was not one of them." I shook their hands and assured them with more confidence than I felt that I would land on my feet and left.

When I called my husband and told him what had happened, he immediately took the rest of the day off work to meet me. We walked and talked but made no plans. I needed some time to just decompress.

That night when I plugged my phone into the charger, I noticed a message from a number that I did not recognize. It was from a recruiter at another university. She told me that my former manager had forwarded my resume to her and based on his glowing recommendation I could have a job starting on Monday if I wanted it. She said, "Anyone who can be so grateful as they are leaving a job would be amazing coming into one!"

The impact of that moment of gratitude did not end with just a new job, however. I wrote up the account of this incident and submitted it for publication. My story about saying thank you when I was fired was published in *Chicken Soup for the Soul: The Power of Gratitude.*

Deborah Norville, journalist and host of the *Inside Edition* syndicated TV show was one of the editors of that book and she was intrigued by my story. The same month that it was stocked on the book shelves at Barnes and Noble and appeared in Amazon listings I received a call from the studios of *Inside Edition.* I was amazed to hear, "Deborah Norville would like to interview you for a segment on her show."

That one little thank you opened several doors of opportunity for me: a new job position, a story in a New York Times best-selling book series, and a segment on national TV.

Through it all I discovered that gratitude is most effective when least expected. It is a tool that anyone can use to transform his or her life for the better and it costs nothing to implement.

5

Friends with Benefits

"If I loved school at all, I loved it for what it provided me -
access to bonds with people I grew to cherish. And nothing
was better than working toward my dreams alongside
people I loved who were doing the same."
— Liz Murray, author of *My Journey From Homeless to Harvard*

An extremely important aspect of a student's time in
college is the social factor. It is a time to meet new people
and build friendships with people you might never meet
anywhere else. When you arrive on campus you are
starting anew and you can be whomever you want to be,
elevating your status or decreasing it.

Albert, Tommy, and Erich became friends at Harvard. They
were all from different backgrounds and had different
goals for their futures, but each one influenced and
enriched the other's lives for decades.

Albert came from a political family. His dad was a U.S. Senator for Tennessee and served for 18 years. Albert wasn't strong academically in high school, but his father had the connections to get his son the recommendations he needed to attend the ivy league school.

Tommy met Albert on his first day of college. He came from Texas and didn't know anyone. His family did not have the kind of money needed to pay the tuition at Harvard but his hard work, both in the classroom and on the football field, contributed to his receiving a need-based scholarship.

Tommy and Albert joined a country music band as a way to attract girls, but neither became country music singers.

Albert had intended to major in English but switched to government. He campaigned for the freshman student government council and was elected president. This buoyed his interest and he ended up pursuing politics as his career. Albert, or as you know him, Al Gore, eventually became the Vice President of the United States as Bill Clinton's running mate.

Tommy's interests were very different than Al Gore's but he also had a drive that could not be stopped. In his senior year he was not only nominated as first team All-Ivy-League offensive guard but he also graduated cum laude.

He never took an acting class, but Tommy chose to stay on the east coast to try his abilities at acting. He auditioned for and earned his first role in the Broadway production of "A Patriot for Me" ten days after graduation. This ran for 49 performances and opened the doors for him to get an agent and pursue many more acting roles.

Another of Al and Tommy's friends, Erich Segal, is best known for his novel *Love Story* that was also made into the Oscar winning movie of the same name. He began his life in Brooklyn as the son of a rabbi. He was working on his doctorate in comparative literature when he met Al and Tommy.

By the year 2000 when his former roommate Al Gore was nominated for the presidency, Tommy Lee Jones had become a famous actor and offered his services to speak about Al Gore at the Democrat National Convention in Los Angeles. He began the speech with, "Al Gore has been one of my closest friends since the day we met, on the first day of college, 35 years ago."

Years after their time together on campus Erich Segal revealed that Oliver, the main character in his novel, was modeled after the personality of Al Gore with a little bit of Tommy Lee thrown in. In the movie *Love Story*, Tommy Lee Jones was cast as Hank, Oliver's roommate. It was Tommy Lee's first movie role.

Another student named Irving was teased relentlessly by his roommate about his first name. Instead of recoiling from this annoying person, Irving "sucked it up" and ignored the razzing. As their friendship developed, Irving's friend convinced him to shorten his name to "Ving" and Ving Rhames became his new moniker.

That name that he gained in college has served him well throughout his acting career. He is known for his unusual name and the roles he played in the *Mission Impossible* movies alongside Tom Cruise. If you look up his body of work on IMDB.com just search for Ving. He is the only one who will come up.

Ving's roommate, Stanley Tucci became a well-known actor in his own right. He played the role of Ceasar Flickerman in the *Hunger Games* movies.

None of these students knew who their college acquaintances would become or how those friendships might benefit each other in the future. However, they took the time to develop those friendships. They chose friends who believed in them and motivated them to greater pursuits.

Kate

Kate was waiting in the wings when she stole a quick peak at the audience. Every seat was filled, and she recognized some of her classmates. She felt confident and prepared for the Don't Walk charity fashion show, but nervousness sent a buzz through her veins. She closed her eyes, took a deep breath and let it out slowly. This moment felt like the beginning of something important. She just didn't know what.

When the selected song burst through the speakers she strode onto the catwalk. Holding her head high, she sashayed through the room showcasing a see-through dress with black bra and panties underneath. Kate could feel all eyes on her, especially those of one young man in particular.

The applause reassured her that the audience was impressed. She was gazing over the crowd as she walked when her eyes met those of the young man she'd noticed earlier, the crown prince of England, William Mountbatten-Windsor. Kate felt her face blush.

After the show William waited to congratulate Kate on her presentation. It wasn't as though they hadn't spoken to one another before. They were in the same art history class at St. Andrews and had even eaten together occasionally at the dining hall, but this time there was a connection. It was just William talking to Kate, not a royal to a commoner. They connected enough to share a kiss at the after-party that night.

Although Kate had met William before their days together at college, it was the conversations in the dining hall, brushing shoulders in the residence hall and the commonality of experiencing the same art history course that broke down the walls of social class separation. College leveled the playing field. Little did she know she would one day marry her college sweetheart and become Princess Kate, wife of Prince William of Wales.

Homeless to Harvard

For Liz Murray it was a miracle that she ever finished high school, not to mention being accepted to college. She was raised in the Bronx by drug addicted, alcoholic parents. Her mother Jean suffered from schizophrenia and was legally blind. Jean and her husband had been heavy partiers in the 70s and by the 80s they were addicted to cocaine and heroin.

Her mother received monthly government issued disability checks for her blindness, but within three days of receiving the money it was all gone, spent on rent and drugs. There was no money for food or to even keep the lights on.

Liz says that her parents loved and hugged her, but that was all they had to give. The need for alcohol and drugs took the place of everything else.

Liz avoided school growing up. Her clothes were tattered and dirty and often she had lice in her hair. At school she was mocked and avoided because she smelled bad from not bathing. She felt it was best that she stayed home and cared for her mother instead.

Although she had almost no formal education, she educated herself through her love of reading. A neighbor gave her a set of encyclopedias she had retrieved from a dumpster and Liz read them religiously. It fed her longing for the world outside her roach infested apartment.

When Liz was only 16 years old, her mother died of AIDS. Her mother was buried in a pauper's grave the day after Christmas. Liz's father, no longer able to rely on Jean's disability checks, moved into a homeless shelter. Liz chose to stay at friends' homes, rotating around from friend to friend. She was able to sleep on their couches and eat an occasional meal, but eventually she was asked to move on. Her home became hallways and subways. Meals were found in dumpsters behind restaurants.

Standing in the snow staring at her mother's gravesite, Liz was inundated with memories of her mom. She had always taught Liz to be grateful for what she had, not bitter about what she didn't have. She was a woman who could make others laugh. She lit up a room when she walked in, but the addictions had stolen it all.

She remembered the many times that her mother talked about her dreams for a better life, yet she had never taken the steps to change the downward trajectory on which she was sliding. It was a huge wake-up call for Liz. She realized that her life was a blank slate; it was up to her to make it what she wanted it to be. She didn't want to be defined by her parents' mistakes or her own lonely past.

She said to herself, "What if I woke up every single day and I did everything within my abilities during that day to change my life? What could happen in just a month, a year? What would be different about my life?"

She decided she wanted an education and needed to start by earning her high school diploma. She began knocking on doors and applying to high schools. She did not tell any of the administrators that she was homeless. When she got a "no" she found another high school to ask.

Liz was accepted into the Humanities Preparatory Academy, a high school for at-risk kids and dedicated herself to her studies. She doubled up on her courses and completed four years of high school in two, graduating at the age of 19. She said that she knew she was carving out a new life for herself one course at a time. That dream and the encouragement of great teachers kept her going. When she finished, she ranked number two in her class of 158 students.

With the success of a high school diploma in her hand, Liz wrote an essay applying for a scholarship from the New York Times Foundation. It was focused on students who had overcome formidable circumstances and Liz's story fit the bill. Only six scholarships were given to keep the awards substantial and she was awarded one of them. She just had to choose a college that would accept her. She set her sights on an ivy league school.

She talked about how surreal it was to be applying for welfare at the same time she was applying to Harvard. In the year 2000 Liz, the homeless girl of drug addicts, walked into her first ivy league classroom and sat down next to students from very wealthy families. These became her peers. She says, "I was able to reinvent my life."

In 2003 Lifetime TV released *Homeless to Harvard: The Liz Murray Story*, but the movie doesn't tell the whole story.

After her first three semesters Liz left Harvard to reconnect with her dad. She was able to rent an apartment and take him out of the homeless shelter where he resided. He was clean and sober. She cared for him until he succumbed to the AIDS virus.

After returning to Harvard Liz completed her bachelor's degree and began graduate studies with a plan to complete her doctorate in clinical psychology. Today she travels the world telling her story and urging people to know their "why." Once they figure out why they must do something they will figure out the "how" to get it done. She is married to James Scanlon, her boyfriend from high school and they have two children.

Liz says that all the way along there were people who reached out to help her. She could not have done it alone. As a result, she has dedicated her life to helping others. She often says, "You are not defined by the bad things that happen. You are defined by what you do next."

6

The Power of Connectivity: It's Not Who You Know, It's Who You Get to Know

"Cherish your human connections – your relationships
with friends and family."
— former First Lady Barbara Bush

It was move-in day at the university and Thomas was wrestling a large rocking chair up the stairs of Loyola Hall, blocking everyone else's access. This hall would be his place of residence during his freshman year and he wanted it to be comfortable. Some of the observers scoffed at his endeavor. "What's the chair for? Is your old man moving in with you?"

Thomas grinned. "It's my writing chair," he called back. Everyone on the second floor knew him as the kid with the rocking chair. His room became a central meeting place for deep conversations and hearty laughs, but Thomas was the only one who sat in that chair.

Assigned to the same floor just a few doors down was a student named Bill. The two became friends and enjoyed talking about parties and politics. When the call went out for students to register to run for freshman class president, Bill rushed to sign up. Politics was his passion.

Thomas was supportive of his friend's endeavors, but that pursuit was not for him. Since writing was his interest, he offered to critique Bill's campaign speeches. Bill practiced what he had written while Thomas rocked in his chair, often interjecting helpful phrases, bits of humor and memorable soundbites for Bill to use.

Thomas was a talented writer and found great joy in the pursuit of crafting the perfect sentence to evoke an emotion or compel a person to action. His hope was to one day be a novelist, but his parents envisioned a different path for him. The family expected Thomas to be a participant in the family's lucrative jewelry business. To that end he went on to get his MBA from Harvard Business School. His friend pursued a career in politics.

Working as an executive in the jewelry business enabled Thomas to do writing on the side. Bill was highly ambitious and as he climbed the political ladder, he often called on Thomas to write for him. Bill's charisma coupled with Thomas Caplan's writing skills succeeded in winning Bill the highest seat in Arkansas. At 32 years old Bill Clinton was named the country's youngest governor.

Years later Thomas was again called upon to help Bill prepare for his first presidential inauguration address and then for his second. Thomas was delighted to do these favors. However, their friendship was not one sided.

In 2011 when Thomas called Bill to tell him he had completed his novel and asked Bill if he would read the first draft, the now former president readily agreed. Bill chuckled at the irony. "It was a gratifying role reversal," he said.

The novel, *The Spy Who Jumped Off the Screen,* by Thomas Caplan is a thriller. The hero of the book is an actor who travels the world under the guise of shooting film projects, but whose true intent is to avert a major terrorist attack. Clinton, an avid reader of the thriller genre, was captivated by the story and offered to write an introduction to the book.

That endorsement was gold for Thomas. Had the two not taken the time to get to know each other and build their friendship at Georgetown University both of their future careers might have suffered.

Bill Clinton started a secret habit while he was in college that also propelled his future. He was intentional about collecting connections. Each evening before he went to bed, he listed on 3 x 5 cards the names of every contact he had made during the day. He added the date and time of the meeting, what class they attended together and anything else he thought might be pertinent about that person. Before he returned to the class he would flip through his cards and refresh his memory. It amazed his classmates when he would smile and greet them by name.

Another former president, George W. Bush, had a similar habit that he started while in college. Not only did he write down the names of the people he met, but he added everything he could remember about the conversation they had. Then he would follow up their initial meeting with a personal note or phone call mentioning something the person had told him.

He genuinely enjoyed meeting people and this habit not only helped him to remember each person better, but it also helped him to build a more personal connection. Many people have marveled that when President Bush was traveling through their city, he would make a quick phone call just to say hi. This endeared him to many people and built a strong network of friends and allies.

"Amy"

My husband Tom worked with one young woman who had dropped out of high school because she was not able to read well. She could read individual words but when the words were strung together in a sentence, she could not comprehend the meaning. She needed some one-on-one tutoring.

Tom worked with her over several months until she was able to read and understand her textbooks. She graduated from high school, but that was the easy part.

The difficult part for Amy was that she had stopped believing in herself, that she could fly. Tom taught her how to stretch herself to reach for more. Amy enrolled in college and earned her bachelor's degree, something that had seemed far out of her reach when she was 17 and being coaxed to finish high school.

"Grant"

Another student that Tom worked with had bigger problems than a lack of comprehension. Grant was throwing his life away. He couldn't see the value in himself and his behavior and choices made that very evident.

Tom was introduced to Grant by Grant's parole officer. Working with Tom was a last-ditch effort to save this kid. He would soon be 18 and if he did not change his behaviors, he would be facing serious jail time.

Grant grabbed hold of the lifeline he was given. He turned his life around and became an Emergency Medical

Technician (EMT). He told Tom, "You saved my life and now I'm saving others!"

Discovering and Creating Superheroes

"Amy" and "Grant" are superheroes, but they needed someone to come alongside them and teach them how to use their powers to fly. They had to discover the powers they had. Students have dreams and ideas, but it is critical that they find that one person who can see through their eyes and believe that what seems impossible is possible.

Tom and I have spent many years working with young adults helping them to stretch themselves beyond their own expectations. Our passion is to help college students survive and thrive in college and beyond.

We teach them how to fly above their peers and to stand out as someone truly exceptional. We teach them how to walk through the walls of their campus and connect with the power brokers in their community. We teach them how to become fireproof where they are never without a good job offer. These successes center around making quality connections.

After working with thousands of students one-on-one for years, we decided we needed to create an online training program. Our mission is to help as many students as possible through the "dangerous decade of decision-making" between the ages of 18 and 28 to help them achieve success in college, personal relationships, their careers and in their lives. That's why we created the *College Superhero Secrets* success mentoring program. You can learn more about *College Superhero Secrets* by visiting www.AmericasCollegeAdvisors.com/CSS.

Brad Bird

Brad Bird was born in Kalispell, Montana and after a time his family moved to Oregon. One is a beautiful area within a short drive of the awe-inspiring Glacier National Park. The other is by the coast, but both places have one thing in common - inclement weather. The temperature in Montana is often bitter and cold through the long winter months and the town in Oregon is always rainy.

Brad spent many hours indoors watching cartoons and drawing in sketch books, especially when it was too intemperate to be outside. He particularly loved *Disney's Wonderful World of Color* TV show.

When Brad was eleven years old, he was taken on a tour of Walt Disney Studios. He was shown a flip book of sketches. When the pages were flipped rapidly enough the character on the page appeared to jump up and down and dance. It was a simplified explanation of how the Disney artists were creating animation for the film industry. To Brad they were performing magic and had just revealed the secret formula so that he could do it too.

A friend of the family who had taken an animation course at UCLA explained to Brad how it could be done with a chalk board and a camera. He could draw the chalk picture, shoot the frame, erase it and draw the next image.

When he returned home, Brad could not be deterred from his intent to recreate the magic he had seen at the studios. His dad bought him a used 8mm camera that could shoot one frame at a time which he would need for animation. They worked together to create a stand that would hold the camera still with the lens pointing down at the table. This became Brad's workshop.

He tried the chalkboard idea, but it was impractical. Once the image was erased, he could not recreate it in the same location with the slight changes he needed to show movement. Instead, his dad devised a corner brace that would position his drawing paper in the same place each time under the camera lens.

Brad took his inspiration from Aesop's fable, *The Tortoise and the Hare*, but he added a character twist. He made the tortoise the protagonist thwarting the rabbit's speed and ability to win. He slid one drawing at a time under the camera lens painstakingly shooting each frame. It took him three years to create a 15-minute animated short, but he was proud of what he had done.

His mom urged him to send it to someone high up in the movie making industry to show them what he could do. Her philosophy was to start at the very top. If they said "no" he could send it to the next best person on the list and so on. That way, whenever he got an indication of interest, it would be from the highest he could've gotten.

Although he was only 14 years old, Brad sent his film to the executives at Walt Disney Studios. They were impressed.

The Disney executives offered him access to their greatest minds to apprentice him whenever he could get to California. Brad also had an open invitation to stay with friends in Los Angeles, so he took them up on it. He would travel down for one or two weeks at a time and have his friends drop him off at the Disney studio early each morning while he was there.

Milt Kahl, one of the great animators for the original *Bambi* movie, took him under his wing and gave him assignments that elevated both his knowledge of the industry and his ambitions. However, it was hard for others to believe he could break into the field. In fact, his junior high guidance counselor tried to dissuade him from pursing a filmmaking career. He was afraid Brad's one dream would be shattered and wanted him to have a plan B.

Attempting to open his mind to other options he asked Brad, "If movies didn't exist, what would you do?" Brad answered without a moment's thought, "I'd have to invent them."

Although he took three years off between high school and college, his desire to be in the business of movie making did not go away. He pursued and landed a Disney scholarship to the California Institute of the Arts.

It was at college that he connected with John Lasseter and Tim Burton. Tim Burton went on to create the *Nightmare Before Christmas* animation and *Edward Scissorhands*. John Lasseter became the co-founder of Pixar.

Brad Bird has written, animated and directed several movies including *The Incredibles*, for which he won Best Animated Feature, and John Lasseter, the friend he made in college, was the Executive Producer.

7

B's are Better Than A's

"Your formal education will make you a good living. Your self-education will make you a fortune."
— Jim Rohn

She was running with a determination she had never had before. She had to get away from the darkness that was about to envelope her. As she forced her feet to pound faster, harder, she could feel the tree branches slap her body. Her breathing was heavy and she could hear the pounding of her heart. Her mind whirled with, "What will I say if I'm caught?" Without warning she felt her body fall as though her feet were ensnared in a trap. "What do I say?"

She was jarred awake and a voice broke the silence. "It is a beautiful 75 degrees in Atlanta today. Please stay buckled until we have come to a full stop." Sami was surprised to notice that she was seated with a script on her lap. It was bent and highlighted from hours of study learning her lines. It was a challenging movie role with a lot to memorize. She scrambled to reach her carry-on at her feet and stuffed the script in her case.

"If I'm in Atlanta, it must be Wednesday!"

Overworked Actress

Sami Gayle plays Nicki Reagan-Boyle, the role of Commissioner Frank Reagan's (Tom Selleck) granddaughter on the highly acclaimed TV drama *Blue Bloods*. She also plays the lead role in *Candy Jar,* a movie about a high school debate champion who is fighting to win a college scholarship, but whose teammate seems to be fighting against her.

In 2018 the filming schedules for both projects intertwined which created a chaotic lifestyle, because Sami was also taking college classes full time to complete her degree at Columbia University.

Sami had to be in various locations for the filming of *Candy Jar* (Atlanta, Washington, D.C., and Newnan, Georgia) and then back to New York to film her scenes for *Blue Bloods.* Her schedule was crazy! The movie shoot ran every Wednesday through Sunday for seven weeks. They would finish in the wee morning hours leaving her just enough time to catch a plane at 6 am to be on the set of *Blue Bloods* in time for the Monday shoot. She chose her college classes so that they met in the afternoon and evenings on Mondays and Tuesdays so that she would be able to be in the classroom for the lectures. She confided that she wrote many papers on the plane and struggled to get enough sleep.

Despite all the drama she graduated in 2018 summa cum laude having completed a double major in art history and political science. Although she considers herself a perfectionist, she had to pull back and let some of her work be just good enough. She said, "I learned to remember what's important in life and that doesn't just mean getting an A+ on everything you do."

Most students who enroll in college are aware that grades matter. In fact, many college students are so dedicated to achieving straight A's that they sacrifice other activities so that they will have adequate time to study and earn the highest grades possible. One of my students was so distraught when she earned a B+ in a course that against my advice she insisted on retaking it to replace the B with an A. It was unnecessary and quite frankly a waste of her time.

If you plan on applying to medical school or law school, or even to go on to a master's degree after you earn your bachelor's degree, then working toward a 4.0 grade point average may be necessary. However, if the goal is to launch into a career after completing your bachelor's degree then it is more important to expand your focus from a study only mentality.

Anxiety Attacks

Taylor Hudak, a student at the University of Connecticut suffered from anxiety attacks. She was an athlete, an exceptional student, did volunteer activities and worked several part-time jobs. Taylor was organized, responsible, and dedicated to high achievement. Even when she earned an A on a project, she agonized over whether she could have done even better work.

This excessive drive to excel brought on panic attacks that stopped her from even being able to communicate coherently. The continued personal stress would inevitably lead toward a health crisis. Something had to change. She said, "I decided to value myself over my schoolwork because I was tired of panic attacks."

Taylor chose to build balance into her schedule. She still did her assignments to the best of her ability, but she took more breaks, and made a point to stop her work at 8 p.m. each evening. This change in perspective may have saved her life.

Bill Gate's Regret

Even Bill Gates, who was totally dedicated to his academics says he would have done a little less studying to make time for social activities if he had the opportunity to do his time in college over again. He told the students at Harvard that with all that he has and all that he can buy there is one thing he cannot get at any cost. He buried himself in his studies and wishes he had taken the time for the social experiences that were available to him while in college.

"I never went to a football game or a basketball game or, you know, whatever other sports teams Harvard might happen to have," Gates said. "You know, it worked out in the end, but I missed a lot."

What Happens When the GPA Tumbles?

By contrast Jonathan Sprinkles didn't stress over being the best; he made a point from day one to enjoy his time in college, trying many new opportunities. He was one of those students who stumbled upon his future and he didn't even realize it. He was a marketing major at the University of Texas in Austin. When Tom and I first met him, we were immediately impressed by his warmth, sense of humor and genuineness. He is a natural leader who just makes you want to hear what he has to say. It was no wonder that he was asked to be a student recruiter for his school, specifically for the McCombs School of Business at the University of Texas. It was a great opportunity for him and even though he was not confident about his speaking abilities he accepted the job.

His position set him ahead of his peers. He was no longer just a student; he was a spokesperson and student leader. He was interacting with the Deans of the college. They respected his input and participation. Together they would fly to different cities like Houston, Dallas and San Antonio and present to large groups of college bound students and their parents.

Although he was terribly nervous, each time he took the stage, he pushed himself to be the best that he could be in this role. He explains that he used his nervousness and channeled it into a "high-energy pseudo-comedy routine." He was edutaining before there was even a word for it!

Jonathan brought an excitement to his performance that delighted the Deans and captivated the audience. The Deans would give their presentation about the college and then turn it over to Jonathan, introducing him as the star of the show. He loved it!

Jonathan was doing it right. He grabbed hold of a hidden opportunity that many students would have declined. It was hard to step out of his comfort zone and the idea of adding such a demanding commitment to an already overloaded schedule was daunting. As a result of stepping into this new adventure, however, Jonathan grew in confidence and professionalism and discovered his personal passion of influencing others through public speaking.

Unfortunately, he was doing something wrong as well and it almost completely derailed him. He was letting his studies slide. Speaking was exciting and studying was tedious, so he gravitated to spending all his time getting better at the former and neglecting the latter. Midway through his junior year he had a 1.75 GPA which put him one semester away from failing out of the college.

Jonathan said that he initially felt sorry for himself and berated himself for letting his grades slip, but after some prayer and soul-searching he "decided to live by faith, not just talk about it." He dedicated himself to learning and applying productivity principles and he found the answers he needed to pull up his grades.

He sought out people who were excelling in class and determined to learn from them. He joined their study groups and asked for one-on-one help. He says, "It was my first time ever fully relying on people of different ethnicities and nationalities to pull me out of the hole I dug for myself." He discovered all new opportunities at UT that he had previously overlooked, the programs that the University offered to help students with their studies and they worked.

Jonathan reports that he made the Dean's List for academic achievement two of his final three semesters. He also made some lifelong friendships. He says that being forced to find a way to come back was the "worst best thing" that ever happened to him.

After graduation he worked for Dell Computers as a sales rep in their fastest-growing business division. By 24 years old he was making over $80,000/year, but because of the time he spent recruiting for UT his heart was still in speaking and inspiring others. He felt like he was chained to his sales job because of the good income.

After 2 ½ years at Dell, Jonathan Sprinkles broke free and developed his business as a speaker. He won the national College Speaker of the Year Award several times and is now a sought-after business trainer as well. He makes more in one day than he used to make in one year.

Jonathan's advice for college students is this:

- Get the best grades you possibly can. While your GPA won't fully reflect your intelligence level, it does reflect your ability to stay focused.
- Make friends with the nerds. They tend to do rather well in life (think Microsoft, Google, Facebook).
- The job of your college is to provide you with a quality education and expose you to opportunities to use in the real world. If you are expecting a school to show you why you were put on Earth, you're looking in the wrong place.

Now the title of this chapter is *B's are Better Than A's* because if a student is intent upon a 4.0 GPA, that goal may demand that he or she refuse opportunities like the one that Jonathan accepted. There is often not enough time to do anything else but pursue the highest grades possible if that is the ultimate goal. Extracurricular activities may encroach upon study time and the student needs to organize their time appropriately to maintain a B average.

It is often assumed that people earning a 4.0 grade point average (GPA) will have their pick of high value jobs. This is not true. One of the biggest secrets of the hiring practices of Fortune 500 companies is that they are not looking for people who earned the highest grades or who have the highest IQ. Instead, they are looking for prospects who have high people skills or EQ (emotional quotient). This seems counterintuitive and illogical. Why wouldn't the companies choose the smartest people to join their team?

Companies are looking to hire people who demonstrate collaboration skills and creativity. They want people who will help the whole team succeed rather than those who focus on performing better than everyone else, (the A achievers). In the corporate environment, if you are not able to work with others you will not succeed for very long.

Richard Branson of Virgin Airlines explained his hiring practices and why he chooses people with great personality every time over people with high achievement. "Company knowledge and job-specific skills can be learned, but you can't train a personality."

Bruce Nordstrom, ex-chairman of the department store known for its impeccable service, shares the same opinion, but said it a little differently, "We can hire nice people and teach them to sell, but we can't hire salespeople and teach them to be nice."

LinkedIn data found 75% of all financial professionals agree soft skills are more important attributes for success than technical expertise such as quantitative skills, computer science, and coding skills.

Throughout this book you've been reading about the kinds of activities that other students took part in that gave them an advantage in college and helped to shape their future success.

In the same way, students who participate in our online program, *College Superhero Secrets,* and complete the Action Plans included with each lesson discover that they have an unfair advantage over their peers when it comes to launching their careers. Our purpose for developing the program was simple: to help each college student reach his or her potential and live a life of integrity and purpose.

The program walks you step-by-step through the process of how to capitalize on your time in college. It shows you how to build the right connections and how to take advantage of the right opportunities to build your resume so you can have a career job waiting for you before you even graduate.

Some students stumble into situations that end up being the decisive factor that catapults their career and life into success, but until now, no one was telling college students the secrets of how to do that intentionally or even how to recognize those life-changing opportunities.

Unfortunately, without this guidance too many students' college experiences can be described by this quote from Winston Churchill, "Men occasionally stumble over the truth, but pick themselves up and hurry off as if nothing has happened." Tom and I created *College Superhero Secrets* to change that. It gives you a distinct advantage over your peers and helps you discover your true passion and purpose.

If you want more information about *College Superhero Secrets* go to: www.AmericasCollegeAdvisors.com/CSS

Getting a Degree is Not a Career Plan

Focusing on getting a degree is not a plan - at least not a complete one. Graduating college with a 4.0 GPA will prove you can successfully complete classes, but to ensure you have a career when you toss that mortar board hat into the air you have got to approach your years in school with more than just a focus on grades.

With nearly three quarters of college graduates unable to land a job in their field of study, students must focus on what their future employers really want. The Hart Research Associates Online Surveys of Employers and College Students discovered that "Large majorities [of employers] say they are more likely to consider a job candidate who has participated in an internship, senior project, collaborative research project, a field-based project in a diverse community setting with people from different backgrounds or a community-based project." Employers want people who can show they can work well with others in a team setting even more than students that got straight A's.

So, there is the plan. If you are a job seeking individual, whether in college or not, you need to find and participate in internships, apprenticeships, or volunteer projects and add those experiences to your resume. You may discover a career that fits you before you spend four years studying for a career that doesn't. Something as simple as getting a letter of recommendation from the projects' supervisor will go a lot further toward making you attractive to employers than just having high grades ever will.

8

Don't Take College Seriously

*"Fall in love with the person who enjoys your madness.
Not an idiot who forces you to be normal."*
— Mr. Bean

The whole room exploded in laughter! Rowan Atkinson stood awkwardly waiting for the din to quiet. He was a student at Oxford University completing his Master of Science in Electrical Engineering degree and yet he was being laughed at. Uproariously. People thought he was so funny that tears were rolling down some of their cheeks.

And that was exactly what Rowan wanted.

Rowan had graduated first in his class with a Bachelors of Electrical Engineering degree. Continuing on for a masters in the same discipline is a very demanding path. He found it to be at times tedious and stressful, especially since he had always been a perfectionist. He said, "I have always worried about things more than I should. I always feel that whatever I do, I could do better."

Performing with the *Etceteras*, a revue group of the Experimental Theatre Club (ETC) in Oxford gave him comic relief from the demands of his schooling. It also gave him a career, one that was totally unexpected.

Rowan had always struggled with a speech impediment but he found he could use this to his advantage. His comedy sketches were hilarious and he enjoyed collaborating with people like Richard Curtis, a creative writer he met in college who later wrote many successful screenplays.

Rowan does not say much about his personal life. Whether or not he ever envisioned himself evolving into the beloved quirky character Mr. Bean or having his own show with a global following or becoming a highly successful movie actor (*Johnny English*, *Love Actually*) we will never know for sure. What we do know is that he completed both his bachelor's and masters degrees in electrical engineering and has electrified audiences ever since.

"The older you get, the more you realize how happenstance has helped to determine your path through life."- Rowan Atkinson

John Krasinski

In 2018 Time named him one of the 100 most influential people in the world. However, actor John Krasinski is best known for his portrayal of Jim Halpert, the endearing, mild-mannered salesman on the TV series *The Office*. He won several acting awards for this role, but he had not originally planned a career in acting. He intended to major in English.

"I wanted to be an English teacher. I wanted to do it for the corduroy jackets with patches on the side," he said.

When he graduated from high school, John was itching for an adventure before he got down to the business of college. He chose to defer his first semester of college and immerse himself in the life, the jungles, and the beauty of Costa Rica.

John justified this excursion by signing up to teach English to the locals. It would be a way that he could "try out" a teaching career before he committed to four years of pursuing it. In his free time, he enjoyed abundant new experiences in Central America.

By January he was ready for his college education at Brown University to begin, but the route he had always planned to take had changed while strolling the Costa Rican beaches. He needed to plan for more adventure in his life. He just wasn't sure what that would be.

"When I got to college, as I was walking across campus one day, I ripped off a little flyer for this sketch comedy group. It ended up being one of the greatest things I have ever done."

He joined the comedy troupe called *Out of Bounds*. The troupe became a family of friends and performing before an audience gave him confidence and the awareness of what would make people laugh. It was a rush to hear people applaud and respond to his antics.

Instead of majoring in English and getting his teaching certificate, Krasinski chose to major in theater arts. He continued to hone his skills in English and his writing abilities blossomed. He became an accomplished playwright and expanded his studies further by getting training at the National Theater Institute and studying in England at the Royal Shakespeare Company.

After graduating with honors in 2001 he moved to New York City and got a job as a waiter. This job certainly did not need the degree he had just earned, but it paid the bills. He continued to write and got himself an agent who would notify him of roles for which he could audition. He did readings for off-Broadway plays and began to win his auditions, earning spots in commercials and small roles on TV shows.

At the age of 25 John got the exciting news that he was cast as a regular in the NBC sitcom, *The Office*. Little did he know his acting adventure would actually have him sitting in a desk for the next eight years! Fortunately, during those years, he was also cast in several movies that gave him some variety.

John's writing skills that he perfected while at Brown have served him well, giving him the joy of seeing some of his screenplays produced into popular movies (*Promised Land*, cowritten with Matt Damon, and *The Quiet Place*).

In 2018 he was cast as the lead character in the Amazon Prime series *Tom Clancy's Jack Ryan*. The character is a highly intelligent CIA analyst who, because of his knowledge, is thrown into dangerous field assignments. Although this role has few comedic moments it offers just the type of intense adventures that John Krasinski has sought his whole life.

John's advice: "Always trying new things is always more fun, and it can be scary, but it's always more fun in the end."

Michael Dubin

Not everyone who attempts comedy ends up in show business, but Michael Dubin, founder and CEO of the Dollar Shave Club believes studying it is one of the best things anyone can do. In fact, he has credited his study of improv comedy as the most valuable classes he ever took that catapulted him to his success in business.

Mike had completed his bachelor's degree in history from Emory College and was working full time, but felt he wanted more education. He signed up for evening classes in business, but then discovered *Upright Citizens Brigade* which offered classes in improv.

Improv comedy is a form of theater in which there is no script. The plot is made up on the spot, usually from suggestions given by the audience. It is fast paced and unpredictable. The actors learn how to absorb information quickly both from the audience and from what their fellow actors say and do.

Their challenge is to develop a story, move it forward and be able to change directions on a moment's notice. The results generate not only laughter but also awe that the actors can be so spontaneous and creative. Michael too was awed and wanted to learn that ability. He felt it would help him in business.

His first job out of college was as a page at NBC's New York Studios. His title was Office Assistant to NBC President Andrew Lack and his responsibilities included conducting tours for the general public through the studios. He also assisted in researching and selecting B-roll or background footage for the nightly news stories.

He worked at 30 Rockefeller Plaza, the same place that Saturday Night Live was filmed. His job was to direct the people who were there to watch the broadcast and accommodate the audience's needs. Being able to watch the antics of the SNL comedians was a bonus for Mike.

Mike changed jobs every two or three years. He expanded on his experience and learned how corporate America works from his employers at MSNBC, Time Magazine, and Sports Illustrated. His focus was primarily on coming up with unique marketing and branding ideas. The nightly improv classes, which he continued to participate in for years, kept his mind fresh.

Serendipitously, in 2011 Mike was asked the question, "If I gave you a warehouse full of razors what would you do with them?" Mark Levine (who became the co-founder of his future company) had posed the question at a holiday party where they first met. Mark may have just been making small talk, but he went on to say he had a background in manufacturing and if Mike could come up with a good idea, he knew where they could get affordable twin razor blades.

It was an odd proposition, but as Mike said, "Not all the important choices present themselves obviously as the important ones." His improv training kicked in and he took this on as a challenge.

He first thought like a marketer and later as an improvist. He brainstormed on what the biggest irritations were about razors and wondered if he could create a company that solved those problems.

He wrote down everything that came to his mind: having to pay too much for the little blades of metal, taking the time to run to the store, waiting for a store clerk to unlock the safety case for him to access what he needed and other inconveniences. Mike decided that for one dollar a month his company would send quality razors to the customer's door.

He felt he may have hit upon a solid business concept. He called it the Dollar Shave Club, created a logo and designed compelling packaging, but he had to raise money to be able to launch and advertise his company.

Mike wrote an ad script that incorporated the kind of humor one might see at an improv show, except that he prepared the lines and stunts beforehand. He wrote, filmed, directed and even acted in his commercial. It was laugh out loud funny starting with the line, "Are the blades any good? No. Our blades are f**ing great!"

His video helped him land investment money to get the business started, but when he posted it to the internet the video went viral! There were so many orders coming in that his website crashed and he ran out of inventory in the first six hours. It was actually terrifying and extremely difficult for him at the time.

As Mike told it, "You work so hard for years on this idea that everybody has told you is a terrible idea and suddenly you're about to prove them all wrong, and your wildest dreams turn into your worst nightmare." He feared his company would drown in the tsunami of orders.

Mike managed to solve their problems of too much too soon by bringing in more investors, purchasing more inventory and hiring employees as fast as he could. Despite the potential disaster that the onslaught of new customers brought, he managed to keep the company afloat and did four million dollars in revenue in 2012. The following year the Dollar Shave Club did nineteen million in sales and in 2014 they brought in 65 million dollars, all with just one dollar per month per customer plus shipping.

Just five years from its start-up, the Dollar Shave Club was sold to Unilever for $1 billion dollars. If you ask Mike, "Did learning improv really contribute to your being a successful CEO?" he will tell you, "When you're in meetings with 20 people and decisions have to get made, it really helps to be schooled in a discipline of quick thinking. That's what improv really is."

9

The Clock Is Ticking

"We didn't lose the game, we just ran out of time."
— Vince Lombardi

Frank Abagnale never went to college, but he led a very exciting life. He was an imposter who successfully fooled authorities into believing he was a doctor, a lawyer, an FBI agent and a commercial airline pilot all before he was 21 years old. He was apprehended by police and escaped. Twice. His most harrowing escape was accomplished by crawling through the toilet of an airplane and tumbling to his freedom while the commercial airliner taxied down the runway.

When he was finally thrown in prison for his crimes of impersonating officials and forging checks, he languished there for five years. He was paroled and granted his freedom on the condition that he be a consultant for the FBI, teaching them what he knew about committing white collar crimes. Frank eventually opened his own consulting company, Abagnale & Associates, that deals with financial fraud.

This is not the best way to pursue a career.

College offers the unique opportunity to try out many different occupations without ruining your resume or getting arrested for being an imposter, but this opportunity is only good while enrolled in college.

A journalism student told me she intentionally signed up for a pre-med anatomy course where she was able to help with an autopsy on an actual cadaver. It gave her the opportunity to be a forensic scientist for the day. She said it was a unique experience and gave her an understanding of how murder mysteries are solved. More importantly, she said, it helped her decide to stay with her journalism major. She discovered that one day with a cadaver was enough for her.

Stephen King

As a student, Stephen King was not repulsed by the thought of dead bodies. In fact, he enjoyed crafting horror stories that included detailed descriptions of corpses. He eventually became one of the highest paid authors and has seen more than 100 adaptations of his works become movies or TV series.

However, before King's first novel *Carrie* was made into a blockbuster movie and long before it was even accepted for publication by Doubleday, he had plenty of his writing published in his college newspaper. This exercise of writing regularly and meeting deadlines developed King's writing discipline.

When he was newly married, he and his wife Tabby both had low paying jobs, but instead of getting a second job he continued his commitment to writing every day. King kept a typewriter on a tiny table that was wedged between the washer and dryer in their laundry room. Here he locked himself away and worked on his stories each evening after work.

College may have given him his start but King also credits Tabby for launching his career. Although he sold a few stories to magazines, the rejection letters he received were far more plentiful. He felt it was time to give up his pursuit of becoming a published novelist.

King explains it this way, "There is a time in the lives of most writers when they are vulnerable, when the vivid dreams and ambitions of childhood seem to pale in the harsh sunlight of what we call the real world, in short, there's a time when things can go either way."

When he was at this moment of decision in his life, he had been struggling to flesh out the character of a shy high school girl with telekinetic powers. The teen is mercilessly ridiculed by her peers until she is pushed to exact revenge using her powers. King had completed three single-spaced pages of his story when he crumpled his work in frustration and threw it in the trash bin. He was done!

Tabby, however, while doing the laundry discovered his discarded work and smoothed it out to read it. She became captivated by the story and insisted he complete it. With his wife's encouragement he persevered and *Carrie* was born.

Wendy Williams

Wendy Williams, TV talk show host of *The Wendy Williams Show*, saw her opportunity when she was in college and decided to be a DJ for WRBB, the student run radio station at Northeastern University of Boston. It was a non-paying position for which she had to audition.

To qualify to work at the station she had to take a non-credit class to get her clearance. In the class she was trained how to run all the station equipment and was tested on her knowledge of the regulations of the FCC, the Federal Communications Commission.

Wendy desperately wanted to have her own show, so after completing the required class and passing the tests she created a demo reel of her own unique half hour show. The purpose was to showcase her knowledge of running a radio program and to give the college an idea of what her show would be like. The station engineer approved of what he heard and she was granted her first show.

That student run radio show was the beginning of Wendy's success. It not only gave her hands-on knowledge about the industry but it began her love affair with the medium. Even with the experience listed on her resume, however, it was still a struggle after graduation for her to land her first paid radio position and when she did, the pay was poor.

Wendy stuck by her dream and branded herself as the outspoken radio host who asked the questions of celebrities that no one else would ask. She boosted her fame in 2003 when the Grammy Award winning singer Whitney Houston called in to promote her music.

Wendy pressed Whitney to tell her the truth about rumors of the singer's drug abuse problems. The conversation escalated into an on-air profanity laced refusal by Houston to answer any questions. Wendy calmly talked Whitney's anger back down and kept the conversation going.

Wendy's reputation continued to grow, and in 2009 she was inducted into the Radio Hall of Fame. She had made her mark in radio, but she wanted even more. She made the transition from radio to television and is now the host of her own TV talk show. The Wendy Williams show has continued to be highly watched and highly rated for over 10 years running.

Cavin Gray

Cavin Gray has eaten live bugs, had his hair lit on fire, and been arrested for drunk driving, but only when acting for TV and movies. In real life, when he is not acting, he can be found in full scrubs, standing beside brilliant surgeons as they perform a heart transplant or stem cell procedure.

Cavin is a film producer for Phoenix Children's Hospital, creating documentaries about the children and their families who have had their lives changed by life-saving procedures. Acting is his side job.

Like Frank Abagnale, Cavin finds himself in unique situations often, like the day he was given short notice to board a private jet to document the retrieval of a heart that had become available in a different state. He sat and talked with the surgeons about their thoughts and concerns as the plane flew them on their mission. The heart was scheduled to be given to a sixteen-year-old boy who had only a few weeks to live unless he received a new heart.

The mood that day was intense. Everyone moved quickly as both the life of the boy and the life of the heart were dependent on fast action. Unfortunately, the surgeons determined that the heart was not viable and they had to return to the hospital empty handed.

Cavin was not playing a movie role. This was real life drama that he was documenting and he was burdened for both the family and the doctors who would have to convey the bad news. The family would have to wait longer, hoping and praying for their son to hold on to life.

A few days later Cavin received a call that another matching heart became available. He was told to grab his camera equipment and scrub in for surgery. He was able to witness and record a medical miracle as the teenager was given new life right before his eyes.

A few weeks later he returned to the hospital to film the patient and his parents' personal experiences of how they each dealt with the medical crisis and eventual deliverance. His life is far from boring and it was all made possible because of the choices he made in college.

From the time he was given a small part in a community theater production of *Anne of Green Gables*, Cavin wanted to be an actor. The production was staged the spring before he graduated from the eighth grade and he just knew this was his path. He especially wanted to act in movies or on TV.

When it came time to choose a college Cavin decided he needed to be in California. It was an expensive four-year school and he would have the additional costs of traveling to and from his home in Arizona, but with college loans he could do it and this would put him closer to Hollywood.

His plan was to audition between classes. However, he discovered his first year that many of the audition times were scheduled during his classes. He had to choose to audition or pass his courses.

He decided to wait until he was home for summer break to pursue acting classes. In these classes he was told, "The number one job of a professional actor is to audition again and again and again and occasionally, you will win a part and be paid."

His acting coach wanted him to get his first experience in the industry, so when she learned that the CW network was holding an audition to find the cast members for a new TV series, she insisted that he participate.

Although he did not feel he had the self-confidence yet to pull it off successfully, Cavin memorized and practiced all the lines he was given on his sample script. The character for which he was auditioning was named Eddie and the scene had him seated at his computer sending out a cryptic video message to his friends. Cavin had rehearsed the scene seated at an imaginary computer conjuring up the emotions that the young man was expressing through his words.

He knew his lines and he knew the part, but he was nervous and felt a little sick to his stomach as he drove to his first professional audition. Cavin signed his name at the bottom of the list of actors who were all waiting to be called. One by one each person's name was read and the person was ushered into a closed room. No one spoke as they waited. Cavin's heartbeat quickened as each name was called. He searched the face of each actor that emerged from the room looking for a hint of emotion. Did they feel like they had nailed it?

Finally, it was his turn and he felt that the most important thing he could do would be to convince the casting directors that he knew what he was doing.

"Stand on the tape mark on the floor and state your name, then begin your audition," said one of the judges. He noticed the red light on a video camera pointed at him and registered that it was silently recording his every move.

Cavin looked down at his feet to make sure he was in the right place and began reciting his lines. He knew the lines perfectly and yet he stumbled over the words. "I blew it!" he thought, but quickly asked, "May I try that again?" The director gestured for him to go ahead, so Cavin turned his back to them, walked a few steps and wheeled back around to start the whole audition over.

To his horror he fumbled his lines a second time! He realized what was causing the problem and knew he could correct it if he could just make one little change. Boldly he asked for a third try, but this time he also asked for a chair. "Because my character is sitting at a computer in this scene," he explained, "I rehearsed the lines sitting down."

An assistant brought in a chair and Cavin turned around and walked into the room as though it was the first time, not his third time, and he sat down. Instantly he became Eddie and performed just as he had when he was practicing in his own room at home. He was disappointed that he hadn't performed like this the first time.

He thanked the directors for their time and left the studio feeling like he needed to apologize to his acting coach. He had wanted to make her proud, but felt he had failed miserably. No one asks to redo an audition three times!

The next morning his acting coach called him to give him the news. He knew he hadn't gotten the part and said, "I think I forgot everything you taught me." She chuckled and told him that it was indeed a bit of a disaster and confirmed that the part of Eddie was not his. However, she said his do-overs definitely made him memorable. The casting directors called him "the turn-around kid" and they absolutely wanted to hire him for a different role in the same series.

Bolstered by that first win and yet sobered by how easily an acting job could be lost, he transferred to the local community college so that he could reduce his college loans. He knew that if he wanted to make a career of acting, it might be some time before he was making a lot of money. He didn't want debt to force him into a full-time job that would prohibit his taking time off to audition.

Before he decided to transfer, he took a tour of Scottsdale Community College. He was shown the movie making equipment room. It was affectionately called "the cage." The equipment inside the barred room was very expensive so it had to be kept locked up at all times with a guard inside. With his college ID he would be allowed to check out state of the art cameras, lights, boom microphones and camera dollies. His mind exploded with creative ideas. He wanted to learn and utilize every tool that was made available to him.

The students in his film class were each required to create at least one movie and every movie required a team to make it happen. Cavin signed up to be on every team. He didn't care what role he was asked to play, he eagerly did it.

His weekends and evenings were dedicated to film projects. Sometimes he was an actor and sometimes the director. He filmed scenes from behind the camera acting as director or cameraman and in front as the actor. Other times he searched out locations for the shoot, set up scenes or covered the responsibilities of the grip or gaffer.

The film shoots often ran throughout the night with him returning home with only enough time to shower and change clothes and head to his morning class, but he loved it all!

Cavin has since appeared in several TV commercials, in feature movies and independent films. He recently told me that he has a reputation in the industry of being a dedicated professional.

He credits the time he spent in college working on all those projects as one of the main reasons for his success. He was intentional about learning everything he could, both in the classroom and in the student projects and that gave him experience beyond his years.

Recently he was on a movie shoot with Pure Flix Productions. They were producing the *Case for Christ* movie and Cavin was hired on as the Producer of the EPK, the Electronic Press Kit. Simply stated, his job was to create the "bonus extras" that would be available on the DVDs.

He was thoroughly enjoying this responsibility. He got to talk with the actors as real people. His job was to interview each one and get their thoughts about the movie on film.

Mike Vogel, the lead actor who played the role of journalist Lee Strobel talked openly about his experiences on set and with other projects like the TV series *The Brave* and *Under the Dome*. Off camera they laughed together about the prank the film crew had played on him while he was taking a nap in his movie trailer. When Vogel stepped outside, he was surprised to discover the crew had built him his own wooden deck! Mike even razzed Cavin about crashing a drone camera he was piloting during a shoot.

Everything seemed to be going well when three weeks into the making of the movie, the director told Cavin, "We have a problem!" She told him she had not scheduled one of the actors for their interview and that actor had completed her role and was gone. Cavin looked on his chart and assured her that he had done that interview. "How did you manage to get it?" the director asked.

Cavin told her that, because he had acted in films himself, he knew how to read the call sheets for the actors. He took the initiative to read the sheets and determined the best times to schedule each actor for an interview regardless of what was listed on the schedule. He had noticed her mistake and corrected it.

Every college offers their students access to equipment, experiences and opportunities that mirror those found in the professional world. Much of that equipment in the professional world, however, is only available to those who have been trained on it and have experience using it. The student with a college ID that can verify his or her enrollment can get the training and experience that is required.

Once you are out of college that professional equipment is much harder to gain access to or is simply unattainable. You only have a limited amount of time – while you are in college - to have ready access to this equipment.

Take advantage of every opportunity your college provides you while you are still a student to get a jump start on your career. Some of the most important learning you can do in college will take place outside of the classroom.

BONUS: Free eBook
8 Things You Must Know
To Succeed in College

Your college advisor is there to help you get through college to graduation, but just getting your degree is not enough. College is not about getting a degree, it is about getting a career. Learn the 8 things you MUST do *in* college to make sure you have a lucrative career *after* college.

Get your FREE report by going to:

www. AmericasCollegeAdvisors.com/8Things

10

Paid NOT to Go

"I am not a product of my circumstances.
I am a product of my decisions."
— Stephen Covey

Every life is built on a series of choices. It begins at the very moment of birth when every infant must choose to take that first breath of air, a very foreign act after several months of receiving all its oxygen through the umbilical cord.

After that the baby must choose to take in sustenance and to cry out for other needs to be met. To make it successfully through toddlerhood there are a succession of choices and affirmations of the will to live, to stand, to walk and to succeed.

With each new year of life comes bigger choices that steer the direction that one's life will take; to learn to run, to swim, to study, to participate in teams and to make connections with friends.

For most young adults, high school graduation comes with another big choice, of whether to go to college or not. Although tuition is more expensive than it has ever been, financial aid, scholarships and government grants make enrollment accessible to most everyone, but should you enroll?

Sometimes a full paid scholarship will be the deciding factor. If your tuition was fully paid, then why not spend the time to get your degree? You would have several opportunities to choose a career path while taking courses.

But what if instead of full paid tuition you were offered a lot of money to walk away from college, to choose not to go or not to finish? What if that offer was for $100,000 or perhaps more, say five million dollars? Would you take the offer and forget about going to college?

As a theoretical question the answer seems easy, take the money and run! However, for the students I am going to tell you about that was a choice they actually had to make and they did not make the decision lightly.

NFL or Degree

Zach Allen is a man of intense focus. While he was growing up, he got great grades in school even as he excelled in three sports; basketball, baseball and football. During his first year in high school, however, he realized that with his homework becoming more time consuming and sport practices more strenuous he would have to let something go.

Because of the insistence of his high school coach (who told him quitting football would be the stupidest thing he could do) Zach chose not to drop out of football and as a defensive lineman he began racking up impressive statistics. By his senior year football scholarships began coming in and he chose to enroll at Boston College.

Zach's college statistics grew more slowly, but by his junior year the NFL recruiters had noticed him.

As a student at Boston College his peers were being asked, "When are you going to declare your major?" Zach was asked repeatedly, "When are you going to declare yourself eligible for the NFL draft?"

Zach's football statistics were impressive and by the end of his junior year at BC he was named the defensive recipient of the George "Bulger" Lowe Award. This award is thought to be New England's equivalent of the Heisman Trophy. Many professional NFL recruiters had their eyes on him just waiting to see what he would decide, to finish his college degree or go pro.

In 2018 many people were speculating that Zach would be picked up in the first round of the NFL draft and if not, the second round. According to Spotrac.com a second-round pick is likely to receive a contract worth $1.3 million per year! He would be able to walk into the NFL locker room and pull on the professional uniform, pads and helmet he had long dreamed of wearing, but he would have to leave college to do it.

Well-meaning family and friends wanted to help him think through his decision. They offered advice and warned him of possible outcomes of his decision.

"One injury could end your future as a professional football player," a friend pointed out. "You can finish your degree whenever you want but getting picked up in the first or second round of the NFL draft may never be a possibility again."

To the people closest to Zach what he decided was not a surprise. He chose to complete his senior year, graduating in December 2018 before declaring himself eligible for the millions of dollars that a professional career in football might bring to him.

His reasons? He wanted to complete his degree in finance, as that would be one piece in place that would open doors for a career in the distance future. His deep desire was to play for the NFL but what weighed more on his heart that became the tipping point of his decision came from the relationships he had built at the college.

He felt a deep sense of responsibility to his teammates to continue to work beside them helping to reach their mutual goals through all the football games he had left at school. Zach said, "I love BC, I love my friends and wanted to spend another year with them and get my degree. It was a tough decision but I have good people around me — my coaches, my family."

In the 2019 NFL draft, Zach was chosen in the third round by the Arizona Cardinals. "Individual accomplishments only come with team success. It's really all about the team."

The $100,000 Experiment

Unlike Zach Allen, other students faced with such a decision chose to walk away from their college education and this time it was for only $100,000 over a two-year time period.

The Thiel Fellowship is often referred to as the "grand experiment," and was started in 2011 by billionaire Peter

Thiel. Although Thiel earned degrees from Stanford University and Stanford Law School, he earned his billions from co-founding PayPal and being an early investor in

Facebook. He had concerns about the value of a college education weighed against the high amount of debt that comes with it. He believed that if young minds were given the opportunity to start a business or pursue a dream without the burden of college loan payments forcing them into a traditional job, more wildly successful Facebook-type ventures would be launched.

His hope was that by freeing the most brilliant minds from the time-sucking restraints of college and traditional jobs, many of the world's greatest problems would be solved. Thiel's dream was to launch a massive think tank that would discover the cure for cancer or discover a way to mine valuable minerals from asteroids.

To test his theory, in 2011 Thiel sent out a challenge to young people ages 20 or younger stating that, if they would forego college and pursue their own entrepreneurial endeavors, he would pay them $100,000 over two years to help them do it. On the website it is described this way: "for young people who want to build new things instead of sit in a classroom."

Applications from brilliant and talented young people poured in! The chances of acceptance were small as only 20 to 25 young adults are chosen each year, but the very challenge triggered a preponderance of imagination and "what if's...."

Laura Deming

Laura Deming was only 16 and already in college when she became aware of the challenge. She was always considered extraordinary, so doing the unusual by dropping out of college to be one of the first students to accept the Thiel Fellowship seemed right for her.

She was born in New Zealand and home schooled through her young years which allowed her ample time to feed her fascination with math and science. Her knowledge grew beyond her years.

At age 12 when her parents told her they would be moving to the United States she contacted Cynthia Kenyon, a renowned molecular scientist whom she had read about and asked if she could visit her lab at the University of California San Francisco (UCSF). The request was granted.

Deming showed such maturity and interest in Kenyon's work on the genetics of aging that the bio-geneticist agreed to let the young girl work with her in her lab. Deming's job was to assist with the experiments that were being done using tiny worms and graph the results.

This now became her schooling and her passion. Through the experiments they discovered they were able to extend the worms' average lifespan by ten times without the degenerative effects of aging. This could be a significant step toward discovering ways to extend quality life for human beings.

Despite her interest in this project, the prospect of expanding her knowledge drew her to college and at the age of 14 Deming enrolled at MIT. She had completed two years of college when she was accepted into the Thiel Fellowship program and had to drop out to take advantage of the program.

The fellowship operates on the idea that the young adults have freedom to pursue whatever they want. Eden Full Goh, who was one of the other fellows chosen in 2011 said,

"It was hard for a lot of us to adapt. Going from an environment where someone tells you what to do every moment to one where you can do whatever you want." It was a difficult adjustment.

Full Goh confessed that she spent a lot of days wasting time on email. For Laura Deming, however, having grown up with lots of free time she relished the freedom to think through and flesh out her own innovative ideas.

She developed and pitched the idea of creating a venture fund that would support labs and studies like Cynthia Kenyon's to research ways to stop or greatly delay the aging process. With the time and the contacts she was given through the Thiel Fellowship, she turned her idea into the Longevity Fund.

By the age of 23 Laura was already extremely successful, raising hundreds of millions of dollars for age-related research. However, to attribute her entire success to the Thiel Fellowship experiment would be over simplifying the result. It could be argued that Laura Deming had a head start when she began the fellowship. She had already gotten two years of apprenticeship experience in the lab working alongside serious professionals and had also spent two years at MIT.

David Luan

David Luan was 19 when he landed a full paid scholarship to Yale. It was exactly what David wanted. That is, until he got the offer from the Thiel Foundation offering to fund his next two years of exploration into entrepreneurship. Then all his thoughts changed.

"Ever since I was a little kid, my life dream was to start my own robot company," Luan said. "Everything I have been working on was either consciously or unconsciously preparing me for this.'' He left behind his full ride to Yale and dove into the uncharted waters. He was one of the first Thiel Fellows.

John Meyer

John Meyer joined the Thiel Fellowship in 2015. The "grand experiment" had been operating for four years so he was able to research the alumni and see their successes. Nevertheless, it was still a difficult decision to take the leap. Once he made up his mind that he wanted to accept the fellowship, Meyer turned his back on his previous plans to attend New York University and even declined the internship he was offered at Apple. He had his own business to develop.

His risky choice seemed to turn out well for him at first. Through the Thiel Fellowship Meyer was able to pitch his idea to wealthy, connected investors. These were people he would never have been able to meet, much less talk to about his invention had he been just a college student.

He won many of them over and with the financial boost he received, Meyer was able to pour his time into creating the Fresco News app. It capitalized on the trend of everyday people photographing and videotaping everything around them.

His app captured visual content from people who were in the area as a news event happened and made these images available to the mainstream news media. The person who snapped the photo would get paid a royalty if it was used and Fresco News would get a payout as well. His app had the potential to replace full time photo journalists just as Uber had replaced many taxi drivers.

In one year's time the company grew from 3 to 50 employees and by August of 2016 Fox TV had picked up the app as a way to expand their reach nationwide. It looked like this was another successful business in the making!

Fresco News picked up some impressive investors including Ashton Kutcher, but behind the scenes they were having serious financial and management difficulties. Employees were becoming disgruntled. They were working long hours at relatively low pay on the promise that soon they would be receiving raises and benefits. Instead they received notices that their pay checks would be delayed.

In June of 2017 after reporting that a multi-million-dollar deal fell through, Meyer told the employees to go home; he couldn't pay them. Only a handful of executives and volunteers stayed.

So, what happened? Meyer had a great idea. He had been given start-up money and connections with wealthy investors via the Thiel Fellowship. He had two years to build the business without the hassle of keeping a class schedule or doing homework and studying for exams.

Did the business grow too fast or did the CEO lack the necessary business training and job experience to keep it afloat? What if Meyer had taken that internship at Apple or the courses at NYU first and delayed his start-up until later, would his business have had a better chance?

There have been many successes through the fellowship, like Thinkful, an adult education boot camp that teaches coding and technology one on one, or Eden Full Goh's non-profit company Sun Saluter that provides inexpensive solar powered electricity and clean water for third world villages. However, there have also been many other endeavors like Fresco News that did not reach their potential.

Peter Thiel's grand experiment did change the world, just not in the way he expected it to. Many colleges have adopted some of the concepts his fellowship offers. For example, both Harvard and Yale started innovation labs and resources for funding unique start-ups by their students.

The Thiel Fellowship has changed as well. Thiel discovered that he needed to add college campus inspired features to his program, like occasional classes, mentoring and social functions to give added support to his young prodigies.

Some of the fellows that first year struggled with depression having no support group like family or friends around them. One fellow, Nick Cammarata said, "I thought I'd come out and be mentored by Zuck and [Elon] Musk, but there were no classes and no meaningful mentorships. We had no idea how to build a business."

John Murbach, another fellow, complained about loneliness while he was in the fellowship. "I could get access to any CEO or VC, which was great, but I couldn't find anyone to hang out with." Murbach decided to leave the fellowship and returned to Wake Forest. David Luan went back to Yale.

From the many successful businesses that have emerged from the fellowship and the leap in status that the fellows gained, most of the students who chose the $100,000 over college have said they do not regret the decision.

College Worth More than 5 Million Dollars

In 2012 it was splashed all over the news. Seventeen-year-old Olympic Gold medal winner Missy Franklin was faced with a dilemma. Would she turn down an estimated five million dollars to go to college? Everyone wanted to know. Day after day it was as though she had to look at her college enrollment form and a 5 million dollar check for commercial endorsements and she had to choose which one to tear up.

Franklin had proven herself at the 2012 Olympic games. She was only 17 years old and swam away with several gold medals and a world record in the back stroke. Adding to her phenomenal successes she had a delightful personality which made her worth millions in commercial endorsements, but she had to make a choice. Would she go to college or go pro?

If she chose to go to college she would have to abide by the rules of the National Collegiate Athletic Association (NCAA) to be able to swim for the school team. The rules required her to remain in amateur status which prohibited her from accepting any money for her sport.

"The Athlete cannot:

1. Accept payment or a promise of payments (e.g., cash, prizes, gifts, or travel) for participation in your sport.
2. Agree to have your picture or name used to promote a commercial product.
3. Accept such things as gifts, meals, loans of cars, or money from athletic interest groups or people within the athletics program at the University.
4. Be represented by an agent or organization to market your athletic skills or reputation.

5. Receive any benefit that is not available to other students at the University.

If she chose to go professional and accept the endorsements, she could attend college but would have to forego swimming on her college team.

For that estimated 5 million dollars she would be required to speak on national stages throughout the year, pose for advertising campaigns and perform for non-profit fundraisers. Those responsibilities, along with daily training for the next Olympic trial competitions would demand the dedication of a full-time career. There would be no time for college life.

She had long conversations with her parents and coach about what her decision would mean. She now admits that at 17 years old she didn't even realize the significance of 5 million dollars. Her parents told her that if she agreed to it and chose to go pro that amount of money would carry her through the rest of her life.

Her dad cautioned her that if she didn't go pro right then there was the possibility of her stepping off a curb, twisting her ankle and never being a fast swimmer again.

Despite her father's reservations Franklin turned down the money and committed to keeping her amateur status for two years so that she could enjoy her time in college. She chose to attend the University of California at Berkeley.

While at UC, Franklin got the enrichment she wanted. She won many NCAA titles for the college and she built friendships with her teammates that she felt would last for a lifetime.

In 2015 Missy Franklin went pro and allowed that endorsement money to come her way. Although she could no longer swim with her college team, she chose to continue her education in psychology at the University of Georgia where she could train with her former long-time coach.

It is interesting to note that Katie Ledecky, also a multiple gold medalist who is in the record books alongside Franklin, chose in 2016 to forego the millions of dollars in endorsements and enrolled at Stanford University. Neither swimmer said they regretted the decision.

As in most decisions there is not one good and one bad decision. Most choices we make in life are more like choosing between two paths rather than choosing between staying on the path or jumping off of a cliff. Each decision will have its own consequences but sometimes either one can be equally rewarding. The key is to commit to your decision and do the best you can on the road you've chosen.

11
Star Wars: Competition is
A Winning Thing

"The ultimate victory in competition is derived from the inner satisfaction of knowing that you have done your best and that you have gotten the most out of what you had to give."
— Howard Cosell

Tom and Steve were roommates at the University of Northern Michigan. They were star athletes that had been on several teams together in high school, but once they chose to enroll in college, they each needed to decide on their one best sport to pursue.

They each chose a different one. At UNM Tom played basketball in the position of defensive guard. Steve played football and quarterbacked for the Wildcats.

The friends were extremely competitive and created unique challenges for each other, often culminating in a race up a make-shift ski hill to see who would get to the top first. Each one called out his personal sport fantasy as the prize if he won the race. Tom shouted he would become the head basketball coach at Notre Dame while Steve's dream would be to become the head football coach at Notre Dame. These challenges pushed them to be the very best physically that they could be and their friendship proved to be a catalyst for success.

Tom set a record at the college his senior year for the most minutes played in basketball. He was also named a Division II All American player. Not to be outdone, Steve was named Division II All American quarterback three times. He even led his team to the NCAA Football Championship in their division.

The young men's sport fantasies, however, were not realized as neither one ended up coaching at Notre Dame after graduation, but neither were they disappointed. Tom Izzo became the head basketball coach at Michigan State University leading the Spartans to one of the most successful collegiate programs in the country. In 2016 Izzo was inducted into the Naismith Basketball Hall of Fame.

His roommate, Steve Mariucci (nicknamed "Mooch") became the head coach of the professional football team the San Francisco 49ers and later the Detroit Lions. He went on to become a well-loved American sportscaster.

College Competition

The physical competitions that Tom and Steve designed for each other helped to guarantee their future successes, but a college student doesn't have to create his or her own contests like they did. Many colleges offer competitions like the annual one at Colgate University. To encourage entrepreneurship the college runs an annual competition called Thought Into Action (TIA is similar to the Shark Tank® TV show). The students who enter are required to create a unique business plan and present it to a panel of judges.

The year that student Jake Danehy entered the competition he stood before a panel that included the stunningly beautiful actress Jessica Alba, who also founded the Honest Company, and the talented hip hop recording artist and tech entrepreneur MC Hammer.

To say that Jake was nervous was an understatement. The audience consisted of 3,000 of his peers and professors. He had never stood before so many people before, but he was eager to give his pitch.

Jake was in his junior year majoring in geography when he learned that every year 50 billion plastic bottles are tossed aside with many finding their way into the oceans and onto the beaches. This knowledge triggered his desire to find solutions to the plastic pollution. He thought it would be great to create something practical from the discarded plastic waste.

When he talked to his sister Caroline Danehy about his idea she immediately began brainstorming. Since she was very fashion-minded she thought about different lines of clothing, but making it from recycled plastic might not be very practical.

She spent some time researching and found companies that made polyester fabric from discarded plastic bottles. After getting sample swatches they discovered that the fabric was very soft and when washed it dried quickly. It would be perfect for swimwear. They could sell a product for people to enjoy the beach while saving the beaches as well. It seemed like the perfect solution.

Jake entered their business idea into the competition at his college with the brand name Fair Harbor Swimwear. Caroline was still in high school so she could only watch and wait for the judges' decision. In his presentation Jake emphasized that one boardshort would use eleven recycled plastic bottles. Each pair of swimwear would help to keep the ocean clear of plastic debris.

After asking several questions and passing around the fabric swatches the panel awarded him the prize money. Jessica Alba especially loved his idea since her company is focused on "green" or non-polluting products as well. Jake won startup money totaling $20,000.

The siblings asked another friend, Sam Jacobson, who was majoring in entrepreneurship at USC to help them with all the business details. He showed them that they would need more capital to buy the fabric, hire seamstresses, and pay for marketing, so they launched a crowdfunding campaign. This is an online system of raising money for creative projects that does not need to be paid back. (Our book *Cash for Creatives: Found Money, Fast Money, Free Money* explains in detail how to run a successful campaign and avoid the pitfalls.)

They raised an additional $25,000 and their business was born. It took quite a bit of marketing to build their clientele, but today Fair Harbor clothing is a successful business, an idea that was born first from a geography course and nurtured into being through a college competition.

Carrie Underwood

Jake, Caroline and Sam had a thriving swimwear business before they ever completed their degrees because Jake took the chance to enter a competition that his college offered. Unfortunately, not all colleges offer this type of competition. Sometimes students need to venture off campus to find unique opportunities that will launch them to success.

One of the most famous competitions that lures many college students is *American Idol*. Carrie Underwood was a student at Northeastern State University in Tahlequah, Oklahoma studying mass communications with an emphasis in journalism. During the summer break of 2004 she auditioned for *American Idol*.

If she did not receive enough votes from the audience in any given week, she would have been forced off the TV show. Carrie, however, won the nation's love and votes each week and continued to move through the competition. She had to delay the completion of her college degree because when her fall classes started up again, she was still in the show.

That pause in her college pursuit was worth it. In 2005 she landed the grand prize of a million-dollar recording contract, a Ford Mustang convertible and the use of a private jet for one year. She doubled back and completed her degree a year later.

It seemed as though Carrie came out of nowhere when she appeared on the *American Idol* stage. The truth is that *American Idol* was not her first competition. She had entered several beauty pageants, including one at her university. She was even chosen Miss NSU runner-up in 2004. She had been unknowingly preparing herself to step in front of the cameras to perform for her growing fan base of millions of Americans.

Not all competitions will change a student's career trajectory like it did Carrie's, but every entrance into a competition, whether the student wins or loses, stretches that student's abilities and personal confidence.

Tom L. Schneider

Tom L. Schneider, the co-author of this book, was at Wheaton College majoring in communications when he noticed a flyer announcing a singing competition. It was posted on a bulletin board in the hallway of one of the campus buildings. He thought it might be fun to see how he stacked up to the others who would be auditioning for it. Tom enjoyed singing and knew he had a good voice but had only sung in choirs. He said, "I didn't give it much thought; I just signed up and showed up."

The audition itself was very informal. There was no stage, just a single microphone on a stand stationed next to a piano. A pianist was seated, poised and waiting to play when instructed. There were three judges sitting in folding chairs. An assistant walked up to Tom and handed him three sheets of music and said, "When you are ready, state your name and the title of the piece you have chosen to sing." Tom read through each sheet of music and selected a song he recognized as one he had sung before.

The pianist was given the cue to begin. Tom took a deep breath during the prelude, focused in on the music and mentally blocked out the presence of the judges. He imagined he was singing in the room by himself and belted out his song. He had never auditioned before.

After he completed the final note he watched as the judges wrote things down on their pads of paper. They talked quietly amongst themselves, comparing notes. He tried to determine whether or not they had been pleased with his performance. He stood awkwardly waiting to be excused.

After a few minutes passed, one judge stood to thank him for coming to the audition and walked over to shake his hand. He added, "Do you mind if I walk you out?" When they reached the hallway, the judge told Tom he had impressed them with his voice and command of the music. He invited Tom to be a soloist for his worldwide tour with the Continental Singers. They would be traveling the world performing concerts throughout the summer. He assured Tom he would be back home in time for the fall semester.

It was a thrill to be chosen and Tom's heart quickened as he thought about the possibilities, but he asked if he could have a few days to think about whether or not he would accept this offer. His concerns were many.

First, this was a completely volunteer endeavor. He usually worked through the summer months to help pay for college. Secondly, he would need to quickly raise the money needed to pay for the flights and some of the other expenses he would incur on the trip. His family was not wealthy and could not afford what he needed to participate. His final concern was that he had never performed on a stage before.

He read the materials that the judge had given to him. He learned that if he joined the team, he would be traveling with 24 other singers and 12 instrumentalists to four different continents. The singers would be singing as a choir with only a handful of students performing solos. He would have the honor of being one of those soloists. Before the weekend was over, he had decided to accept the offer and would figure out how to raise the money later.

When the semester of school ended, he met his new summer family, the members of the Continental Singers and together they boarded a bus to begin the journey. The group traveled throughout the United States, to South America, Europe and South Africa. They performed 98 concerts in 93 days that summer and travelled over 26,000 miles by bus, train and plane. The auditoriums at most of their venues were filled to standing room only.

One of Tom's biggest thrills was performing in an arena in South Africa that seated over 5000 people, the very same stage that had headlined Frank Sinatra, Tina Turner and Rod Stewart. He said that after one of his performances, a man from the audience came up to him with tears in his eyes. He said, "I just had to thank you. Your song and what you said, it changed my life."

That summer did not give Tom the desire to pursue a career in entertainment. However, he did use his musical talents for a time to write music and record songs for commercials. Years later he had the honor of singing the national anthem at a major league baseball game. He is currently writing lyrics for a musical.

If Tom had not had the courage to challenge himself at the audition, he would have missed out on an opportunity that only a few others have experienced. Tom says, "Entering that competition taught me that you should challenge yourself to take chances, to dream bigger, and take opportunities that are available to you. You never know what your future may hold when you strive to compete, even if you are just competing with yourself."

12

Fail to Succeed

"Don't worry about failures, worry about the chances you miss
when you don't even try."
— Jack Canfield

"I am worthless," mumbled Alan. I was shocked to hear
this negative personal assessment from a college student
who had always exemplified professionalism and
potential.

"Is this about your math class?" I asked. He had gotten a
poor grade on his previous test and several of his
assignments had not been turned in. He was at risk of
failing the course.

"No, not that." He said.

"What's going on?" I gently pried.

Alan had always been very articulate but now he stumbled
over his words. "I just came from the courtroom and the

judge told me I would never be a productive member of society."

I knew Alan had an incurable, degenerative disease that caused him physical difficulties, but I did not know how bad it had gotten for him. He told me that because of the judge's ruling he would be on disability for the rest of his life. College didn't seem to matter anymore. In fact, he didn't feel his life mattered any more.

As he poured out his heartache, I heard not only the pain, but also his broken desire to be of value. I searched for the right words to catch him from falling any further into despair.

"The judge lied to you," I softly responded.

"How can you say that? I have nothing to offer anyone!" he snapped back angrily.

"You have an amazing voice," I pointed out. "I have always enjoyed our conversations. You are intelligent and well spoken. Have you ever thought of a career in public speaking?"

I thought about how others had used their experiences to bring awareness to a disease or difficulty. There are organizations that would eagerly hire a young man who could speak eloquently about the challenges he was facing on a daily basis.

Alan would have none of that! He did not want to be defined by his disease.

Still, I persisted, "How did you do in your speech class?"

"I barely passed with a low C," he replied.

That surprised me. When I asked why he got such a low grade he said that he got high marks on his oral presentation, but because his hands shake so badly, he was not able to type or write out the speech. The professor marked him down for not having the speech on paper for her to grade. Now I was impressed! To be able to give a full-length speech without notes is very unusual. He had a gift. Alan grunted.

"Humor me," I continued, "If you were given the opportunity to speak before a crowd, what would you enjoy talking about?" What he answered was not at all what I expected.

Alan told me of his fascination with American history. He talked about the founding of our nation and shared with me little known facts about the Civil War. His tone raised a bit as he talked and energy came back into his voice. He said that he had memorized the words of many famous people in history and even quoted some to me. He told me how he frequented local gatherings in Pennsylvania where historical battles were reenacted. As he spoke, I became even more impressed with this student.

Finally, he said, "It's funny, but when I was in high school, I worked part time at a retail store and spent all the money I earned buying authentic costumes from different time periods of American history! I have uniforms from both the Confederate and Union armies. I have uniforms from both World Wars. I even have clothes of a mountain man that I got at a rendezvous. It drove my parents crazy!"

Then it was like he had an epiphany, "Do you think anyone would want to hear me talk about American history while wearing a costume from that era?"

This was an exciting thought! We brainstormed about places that might be interested in what he had to offer: museums, elementary schools and colleges. I gave him a couple of websites for him to research that would tell him more about the business of public speaking, like how to write a contract and how to determine the amount to charge. By the time we ended our conversation he had found a new purpose and focus for his life.

I followed up with him a couple of months later and it was a different Alan that answered the phone. He recognized my voice before I even introduced myself. "I am so glad you called!" he said. He proceeded to tell me that he had already given his first paid speech in costume at a local college! He talked on the economics of the American colonies while dressed as a colonial settler. It was so well received that he was referred to another college. Alan already had a second speech booked for the following month.

Alan is still on disability. He may not be able to finish his degree, but his time in college was not wasted. Through failure and tragedy, he found his direction.

NFL Football Player

Unlike Alan, Trent Shelton didn't have any health issues. In fact, he was in excellent physical shape. He played football for Baylor University as a wide receiver and he was good! As a senior he was Baylor's number one receiver and ranked sixth on the Bear's career reception chart. He was determined to play for the National Football League and when he was signed by the Indianapolis Colts in 2007 as an undrafted free agent, he thought his prayers had been answered.

However, in 2008 he was bounced to the Seattle Seahawks and in 2009 to the Washington Redskins. It looked like his professional football career was going nowhere. Trent was accustomed to being the star football player at his college and even though he was still as dedicated and hard working as he had ever been, success in the NFL continued to elude him. When there didn't seem to be any future there, he walked away from his dream.

Trent was raised in the Christian faith and his father was a preacher. Trent had prayed that if God would make him a success in the NFL, he would use his platform of fame to tell others of God's love for them. However, when his career did not unfold as he had hoped he became bitter and felt that God had failed him. He said, "I turned to things that were temporary whether that be drugs, whether it be partying, certain things that filled me up for the moment but at the end of the day made me feel empty again." Depression began to overtake his life and he was angry at God.

He didn't want to be seen publicly because he was embarrassed and didn't want people asking about his football career. He felt like a failure.

As a way of venting he began to create YouTube videos talking about football and how frustrating it was to be in the NFL yet not able to advance his career like he had planned. The videos were his outlet. "I feel like that was my release. Instead of going to certain drugs, instead of going to the alcohol, instead of going to the pills I started releasing my pain through those videos."

The more he talked about what he was going through, the more he discovered through the comments posted on his YouTube channel that others were also going through tough situations and could relate to his pain. There were other athletes who had experienced the loss of their sport like he had, but there was also the man who needed to provide for his family but had lost his job. There was a kid being bullied at school who felt she had no one to turn to. And there was the devastated wife whose husband left her for another woman after several years of marriage.

People were hungry for hope. The desire he had once had in his heart to help other people was rekindled. He believed that God had bigger plans for his life than he imagined he would have in the NFL.

He teamed up with a friend and fellow athlete to write a series of four books to inspire people to focus on the value and purpose of their lives and their relationship with God. His YouTube videos continued to gain viewership and became a video sensation with millions of listeners. He created a life coaching program called Rehab Time that is giving people messages of grace and hope.

His success in college led to failure in the NFL, but Trent will tell you that failure launched a success far greater and more fulfilling than he could ever have imagined.

Commercial Airline Pilot

Five-year-old Susan jumped up and down on her bed and imagined she was flying! Not many women are commercial pilots, but that was Susan Amstutz's dream for her future. She wanted more than anything else to fly an airplane.

In school she would doodle airplanes on the margins of her papers and more than once she was corrected by her teacher to get her head out of the clouds. Ironically that is exactly where her head was. She was a good student, but there were times her mind drifted away from the class lecture because she couldn't clearly see the board at the front of the room. When her parents discovered that her vision was less than perfect, they got her eye glasses.

The joy of being able to see the tiniest leaves on the trees was snatched from her heart when she was told that a pilot must have 20/20 vision. She would never be able to get a pilot's license. Maybe one day she could have her eyes surgically corrected, but for now it was off the table. She let go of her dream, or so she thought.

High school was an exciting time and she was very involved in clubs and band practice. As college drew near on the horizon she began to research where she would like to apply and what she would like to pursue.

Her parents wanted her to attend the local university that had a very good reputation. Her older brother attended there as well. That was the plan, but as she researched other schools, she discovered that the University of Oklahoma offered the unique degree of aviation and that old familiar longing to soar in the clouds began to tug at her again.

She was accepted at several schools but decided to go to one that had the courses that led to pilot licenses. Of course, she knew she couldn't do that. She wore glasses and besides, very few women make it to a level of commercial pilot anyway.

Susan enrolled and chose a major her freshman year. Then she changed it and she changed it again. She just could not let go of the compelling feeling that she just had to try to be an airline pilot. She changed her major a fourth time to the bachelor of commercial pilot program and jumped in with both feet. There she learned that the requirement of having natural 20/20 vision was a myth. The mandate is that the pilot must have 20/20 vision, whether using corrective lenses or not. She was overjoyed!

It was not an easy program and she had to raise more money than she could get through financial aid loans and grants, but she was determined. The accelerated program put even more pressure on her to keep her GPA at a high level so she could stay in the program.

Susan was doing everything right. Besides getting top grades, she was making good friends by volunteering to work conventions and events for the aviation groups. She entered flight competitions and became the captain of the team. The competitions required her to travel to different states. She met aviation students at other universities and made a point to stay connected with them online.

Her professors noticed her dedication and enthusiasm and asked her to be on the student advisory board. This made her an ambassador to the department. She represented the students and was asked her opinion on any changes to the aviation program that they were considering. She also served on the appeals board dealing with integrity violations by the students.

Not only were the professors impressed, but her fellow students looked up to her as well. Susan was seated on the board of the Aviation Club and was voted in as president of the club.

Unfortunately, failure is a respecter of no one and Susan fell prey to this insidious beast. It struck when she was at her weakest. She was facing an extremely tough exam in statistics the same week that she had to test for her instrument license. Two tough exams in one week was something she had conquered before, but this time was different.

She was emotionally distraught from a bad relationship break-up that was throwing her off her game. If that were not enough, her wisdom teeth had become a health risk and had to be pulled, causing her face to swell and her mouth to ache. As she struggled to stay alert enough to study while heavily medicated with the pain reliever prescribed by her oral surgeon, the stress of everything that was going on in her life weakened her immune system. The nerves in her body exploded in pain! She was hit with an outbreak of shingles.

Barely able to lift her head she stumbled through her airline instruments test and fell asleep during her statistics exam. She failed both!

Susan told me, "Failing was the affirmation in my head saying - see, you can't do this." She was halfway through her accelerated pilot's program and now she would be dropped. She was embarrassed and broken and as her friends advanced to the next level she was being left behind. The temptation to drop out of school was great. She could take some time off, she reasoned, work a job for a bit and come back stronger. It seemed like a good plan.

Unsure of what to do, she tentatively approached her instructors and began to build a plan. Although her failures were significant both of her instructors agreed to work with her. It was not because she was adept at pleading her case. It was because she had already proven herself in all of her previous work. They believed she had the perseverance and courage to get back on track and she wasn't about to let them down.

Susan got the listing of the open office hours for her professor of statistics and made sure she was there every chance she could get. She did her homework there and she studied there. If she had a question he was just across the room and she walked over to ask him to clarify things. Because she could prove her medical situation with documentation from both her oral surgeon and her doctor, she was allowed to retake the test she had slept through. This time she passed!

The instrument exam was trickier. She could not retest but she could retake the course so she signed up for summer school. She put in long hours building her flight times and redoing the work required in the instrument test. She prepared and she pushed herself. When she was tempted to slack off so she could spend time with friends she remembered the humiliation of failure and thought, "I don't want to go through that again," and stayed on task.

She completed her course with an A and graduated in 2017 right on track and with honors. Within a few months of graduation, she was welcomed into Sky West and given her commercial pilot uniform but her drive had only accelerated. Susan applied for and was accepted into the United States Air Force as an officer, another area with very few women pilots.

Susan told me that as hard as that year was, she believes that failure brought out the best in her. Many of her friends ran into difficult circumstances and left school planning to return to complete their degree but never did. Failure was the boulder that nearly crushed her, but that she chose instead to use as a stepping stone.

13

Directionally Challenged

*"With everything that has happened to you, you can either feel
sorry for yourself or treat what has happened as a gift.
Everything is either an opportunity to grow or an obstacle to
keep you from growing. You get to choose.*
– Dr. Wayne W. Dyer

College is a time of change. You are stepping into a new
world of discovery. You will be learning about yourself
and what you want the rest of your life to look like. You
will make choices and set your sights on goals. What you
will discover is that no matter how well planned or how
passionate you are your plans can take a radical change of
direction.

Life is Not Linear

When you enroll in college your college advisor will
discuss the list of forms you need to fill out and the
courses you will need to take. It will sound like college
is nothing more than a checklist. You complete a
requirement and check it off. Then you complete another

requirement and it moves you ever closer to the finish line. Once you have completed all the requirements you will be handed your degree and you will step into the career you had planned, or at least that is how it seems.

But here's the catch; the finish line is really the starting line to the rest of your life. What you thought would be a linear path to success will be fraught with detours, disappointments and some disasters that will cause you to rethink your path. Sometimes these detours and disasters will bury the path completely.

I call this secret (that life is not linear) your bulletproof vest. Put this knowledge on and remind yourself of it often so that you are prepared, because unexpected detours will come your way. The circumstances that hit you will sometimes come at you like a bullet out of nowhere and knock you off your feet! You will survive if you remember that unexpected changes are not death sentences, but rather opportunities to see where else your life will take you.

You will get bruised or even scarred, but these unexpected hits will not kill you. You will be able to get back on your feet and be stronger than before, knowing you can survive whatever comes your way and you will be better for it.

There are three college students I am going to introduce you to: Sara, Chip and Bernie. Each one has their own unique story that I believe will inspire you.

Broken Heart

Sara was never a very popular girl growing up. In fact, when she was in grade school, she was often picked on for being overweight. She spent a lot of time alone and found enjoyment in singing and writing by herself. However, as she grew older, she auditioned for and landed a role in the local theater productions. This began to build her confidence and give her delight. The theater people were very accepting and encouraging, almost like a second family. Unfortunately, when the show ended, so did those relationships.

Her day to day life became more disheartening when her parents announced their divorce. She needed their support as she was still being taunted at her school, and the cruelty of her peers only got worse. Finally, in exasperation over Sara's complaints, her mom gave her the option to change schools and Sara jumped at the option!

This was an opportunity to start over and she made the most of it. Although still afraid of being ridiculed she tentatively ventured into the world of making social connections and caught the eye of the star of the football team at her high school. He also shined on the basketball court and was the kind of guy that she thought would only date cheerleaders.

He started asking her out. Sara was only 16 years old and thought she had died and gone to heaven! This seemed too good to be true because now she was accepted and even envied by the other girls. Sara and her boyfriend went to parties and sporting events together. Every chance they had the two met between classes or spent their lunch breaks together, just laughing about nothing. She says she became intoxicated by the feeling of loving someone and being loved in return.

Looking back, she says there were things that weren't perfect about their relationship, but at the time Sara would not look at those things. She was fixated on this guy.

In their senior year the relationship began to cool off. They had fights and she had bouts of moodiness that continued to unravel their relationship. Sara found that the more her boyfriend pulled away from her the more jealous and controlling she became. This only drove him further away.

In the fall she headed off to UCLA while he stayed in their hometown of Eureka, California. Sara believed that their relationship would survive the separation and be better for it.

When Sara returned home from her first semester at college, she learned the awful truth that her boyfriend had been seeing someone else. This news created a physical pain and anger in her heart. She lost it! Her rage was like nothing she had ever experienced before. She was mostly feeling betrayed that neither her close friends nor her boyfriend had the courage to tell her what had been going on.

After driving to her ex-boyfriend's house and yelling the most awful things she could think of at him, she went back to her home to sob. After a time, she turned back to the comforting habits of her youth and began to pour her thoughts onto paper.

She wrote about how she felt pulled into his presence as though he had a gravity field that was drawing her to him. She wrote that she wanted to be set free from his force field. When she had written the words that were bursting from her broken heart, she put music to them and called the song *Gravity*.

Sara returned to UCLA and completed her degree in communications, but her desire for the passion and comfort that music brought into her life was lit! She

became a member of the campus a capella singing group. She also became friends with the band members of *Kara's Flowers* who later changed their name to *Maroon 5.* She taught herself how to play piano. Her song, *Gravity,* was recorded and featured on the *Best of College a Cappella 2004* compilation CD.

Upon graduation she worked as a waitress and began doing gigs singing and playing piano in bars. She worked hard trying to find her way into the music industry and connecting with other musicians. Because she had not majored in music, she had to learn the language of the industry so she could better communicate with her band members. She saved up all the money she made to buy more recording time at studios and finally produced her first CD to sell at her gigs.

Singer songwriter Sara Bareilles said, "I am grateful to the boy who broke my heart for the very first time. This song, [*Gravity*] gave purpose to all that pain for me and somehow made it feel complete." *Gravity* was birthed in a time of pain and loss and years later it is still one of the most requested songs she has ever done.

Sara went on to win an Audience Choice Award and has been nominated for several Grammys. She has written a book that hit the New York Times best seller list and the songs for a Broadway musical called (ironically) *Waitress,* like her first job out of college.

Broken Dream

Chip grew up living and breathing baseball. He loved the

sport and it consumed his life. He played on tournament teams and school teams. He played every chance he got. He absolutely loved the game, everything from the smell of the freshly cut grass on the baseball field to the scent of his leather baseball mitt. He loved the sound of the crack of the bat hitting the hard, red-stitched ball. He loved the feel of the leather glove on his hand. He worked diligently so that he would be great at the sport.

Many kids in America play baseball at some time or another. It is, after all, the country's favorite pastime. Chip played all through grade school and earned a spot on his high school team. The competition became much tougher by age 14 and yet he continued to excel at the sport.

Several of his former teammates dropped out of baseball or were cut from the team as it became more demanding, but Chip just pushed himself that much harder. He practiced with his dad and practiced with the team and he practiced on his own. He knew the odds of getting on a college baseball team were very small, - only 7 out of every 100 kids who try out make it - but that is all he ever wanted to do: play baseball and go pro!

He enrolled at Northlake College and landed a position on the baseball team. Chip thrived playing college baseball! He transferred to Baylor University choosing to major in business and continue playing ball. When the fall training season started Chip was back in his cleats running, batting, fielding and loving his life. Everything was right on track, a straight line. His life was going just as he planned.

And then he was cut from the team.

Just like that, his dream of becoming a major league baseball player vanished. He was stunned, devastated. He hadn't seen it coming.

He struggled with a deep sense of loss and grief. This was the death of his dream. He said he thought about dropping out of school and spending all his time just playing *RBI Baseball* on the computer but knew that wouldn't solve anything. Friends and family offered lots of well-meaning suggestions, but nothing they said lifted the depression he felt. He was stuck in this funk for about a year.

"Apparently there's a cap to the amount of self-pity time a person gets," said Chip, "because one morning I woke up and realized it was time to snap out of it. The time had come to get on with my life."

Shortly after that day as he sat in a business lecture allowing his mind to wander, he smelled the familiar sweet smell of freshly cut grass wafting in through the classroom window. He watched the landscaper on the riding lawnmower and thought about how this guy was *doing* business rather than learning all the hypothetical things *about* business. He had to talk to him!

At the close of the class Chip ran out and talked to the landscaper, asking him every question he could think of about his job. He applied to work for that same company while he was completing his degree. When he had proven himself to be a highly responsible employee the owner took him aside and encouraged him to start his own business.

Chip took his advice and launched a modest landscaping business. He hired several employees to help with the labor so that he could expand the business and still complete his degree. When he had success with that, he used the courage he had learned on the baseball field and applied it, along with the business smarts he learned in college, to launch several more successful businesses. He took risks and took out loans and tried new ventures.

Not every venture was successful, but each time he faced a setback or financial loss he picked himself back up, put on his business cleats and stepped back up to the plate to take another swing at life.

Most people today know him as Chip Gaines, co-host with his wife Joanna of the TV show *Fixer Upper*. On the show the two work together showing the audience how they renovate and landscape various homes. The show *Fixer Upper* was the second most watched cable telecast of the second quarter of 2017, just behind *The Walking Dead*. They drew over 5 million viewers!

Chip in his book, *Capital Gaines,* says, "I never, ever thought I would say this, but it is the truth: if I could go back in time and have my life work out differently – not getting cut from the team and actually making it in baseball – I wouldn't do it." He went on to say, "Every ounce of energy you invest in pursuing your goals will help you grow toward God's plan for you... even if you end up somewhere you hadn't counted on."

Broken Body

In every high school the students seem to congregate in specific groups. There are the athletes, the math and science geeks, computer nerds and finally, artists and musicians. Bernie was of small stature and not terribly athletic. Math and science did not interest him and quite frankly, when he was in high school computers had not yet become available in the school system. In fact, personal computers had not yet been invented. He found his spot among the musicians. He played the trumpet and his intent was to play professionally.

Bernie was raised by a single mom. His mother's income was barely adequate to pay their bills so he did what he could to help out. Bernie worked at a local printing company. The shop only did very large projects. It was a strenuous job, managing tons of paper and gallons of ink. The machines were loud and the hours long, but the paycheck was good.

Bernie chose his college based on the music program. After graduation from high school he did all the necessary paperwork for admission to the college and focused on his summer job at the print shop.

Then one sticky, hot summer day Bernie's mom received a call that there had been a terrible industrial accident at the print shop. Bernie was being rushed to the hospital. She arrived to learn that three of his fingers on his right hand had been chopped off. The doctors were unable to reattach them.

Bernie would never play trumpet again.

Bernie went through the stages of grief over the loss of his fingers and loss of his life's plan to be a professional trumpet player. He withdrew from the college where he had never been able to start. He struggled through denial and anger, but when he moved to the stage of depression, he became stuck. He could not seem to move on. His mom and his high school girlfriend did everything they could think of to cheer him and encourage him, but he slid into a deep pit of despair.

His doctor enlisted the expertise of a physical therapist to try to help Bernie discover the things he could do without his fingers. As part of the therapy he was urged to get some art supplies and try painting. He could still manage to hold a brush.

The more Bernie worked at his exercises the more he could manage. His mood began to lift and he found he actually enjoyed painting. He had never had any formal art training, but this applying of paint to canvas captivated his interest.

He enrolled at Washington University and studied art. His talent astounded people and upon graduation he was hired by the largest and most prestigious studio in Detroit to illustrate cars for advertisements. Bernie didn't just paint images of cars, he romanticized them and made them compelling. He gave them a mystique and intensity that a photograph could never do. Bernie's incredible talent pulled in additional major accounts for the studio.

Within a few years Bernie moved to Connecticut and opened his own studio. He was no longer painting cars, but portraits of well-known people, landscapes and sporting events. He became the premier illustrator for magazines such as *Redbook, McCall's, Sports Illustrated* and many others. He painted the portraits of several U.S. presidents including John F. Kennedy, Jimmy Carter and Ronald Reagan. He was commissioned to do the artwork for four U.S. postage stamps and he painted the portraits of many famous athletes and celebrities.

I had the opportunity to attend a week-long workshop taught by Bernie. I couldn't wait to meet this amazing artist in person. I had followed his career and collected the magazines that published his illustrations for years. When we spoke, I noticed he had a habit of keeping his right hand hidden in his pocket as though his finger stubs still embarrassed him.

The loss of his fingers was indeed a tragedy. However, if the accident had never happened, he might never have discovered his magnificent gift of painting.

Bernie Fuchs (Fewks) was the youngest artist to be named to the Society of Illustrators Hall of Fame. He married his high school sweetheart and with her raised three children. He was the highest paid illustrator of his time and won many awards.

The accident made him believe his life was over, but it was a new beginning. Bernie had to choose to start again in a whole new direction and he blessed the world with his talents.

Your bulletproof vest is to remember that life is not linear. Things will happen that force you to change direction. Circumstances may steal your biggest dream from you, but you can dream again, and even bigger.

Just like Chip, Sara and Bernie there will be circumstances in your life that may feel like bullets to your chest. These events may make you feel like a victim. They may completely change the trajectory of your life, but if you work within the new parameters of your situation you can stand up and remove the bullets from your bulletproof vest. Lay aside the feelings of loss and move with expectancy into your new reality.

Watch for and choose even bigger dreams than the one you left behind. As Zig Ziglar often said from the stage at his speaking events, "It is not what happens to you that determines how far you will go in life; it is how you handle what happens to you."

14

You're Not the Problem – Find One

"At the end of the day, it's not about what you have or even what you've accomplished. It's about what you've done with those accomplishments. It's about who you've lifted up, who you've made better. It's about what you've given back."
— Denzel Washington

"I just can't do this," Jasmine told me when I called to check on her progress in her current courses. "I don't know what I want to be or how I can possibly get there." She was on the verge of dropping out with no plan for her life. She had always risen to the top of her classes in high school but now she was frustrated that she was not excelling in college. She felt that there were so many students who were much more capable than her. How could she ever get noticed as an achiever?

I had heard this frustration expressed by many other students during my years as an academic advisor. The American College Health Association (ACHA) reports that six out of every ten college students struggle to overcome feelings of extreme anxiety, especially during their freshman year. Many students become so depressed they can hardly function. The majority of students who drop out of college do so in their second year.

Although I am not a psychologist, I can tell you what many of the students with whom I have worked confided to me. Like Jasmine, there is the fear of not being good enough. There is the overwhelming feeling of losing ground if they stop for one minute to catch their breath.

They compare themselves to others and are afraid that they will not be able to land a good job. Many students have told me, "Everyone else is much better qualified (or skilled or appealing or _____) than I am. I'll never succeed." They begin to drown in feelings of inadequacy and focus on their desperate need to fix themselves.

I tell them that their drive to be the best is commendable, but their focus is misdirected. Those same students who choose to redirect that "fix it" focus on a bigger problem outside of themselves often find that their personal problems fix themselves.

Not Enough Copiers

Paul Orfalea (OR-fah-la) genuinely had problems. He could barely read and he couldn't sit still. He struggled with dyslexia and ADHD, attention deficit hyperactivity disorder. Because he could not keep up in his classes, he chose to be disruptive. Many teachers felt he was incapable of learning. When he finally graduated high school, he was ranked 1192 in a class of 1200. That's 8th from the absolute bottom. As he tells it, "I still have no idea how those seven kids managed to do worse than I did."

Paul was raised in a strong, supportive family of entrepreneurs, but he did not gain self-esteem as a child. In fact, even though he was tested and found to have a high IQ of 130 (an average IQ is considered 90 to 110) he was the kid who was singled out to be laughed at and called stupid. He was expelled from four different schools. He once overheard some family members discussing that he would never be employable.

Paul explains that he had a different way of processing information and that his mind was highly creative. Because of that creativity he found different ways to accomplish his assignments, and often that meant that he enlisted the help of friends or family.

What gave him hope was the realization that once he became an adult, he would be able to specialize in only what he was best at doing. He would not be required to be good at every subject as is required in a school setting. Instead of obsessing on fixing his weaknesses he found people who were strong where he was weak and befriended them. They became his success team.

He enrolled at the University of Southern California and just squeaked by. His best grades were the result of team projects. But Paul was blessed with one attribute: he had the ability to memorize things quickly. He had developed this skill over the years because he was not adept at writing things down. He also had a mind for "what if?"

Paul was always observing and thinking creatively about his surroundings. What could he provide that others needed?

During one assignment at the college his senior year he needed to run to the copy center on campus to print out multiple copies for his team members. It was the spring of 1970 and the copiers were in high demand that day due to the law students printing out information about the notorious Charles Manson murder trial.

Paul was not irritated by the long lines. As he waited, he watched in awe at the volume of business that was flying through that office and thought, "What if I opened a copy shop near a college that didn't have one?" And he knew of just the place, the University of California, Santa Barbara where his girlfriend went to school.

He completed his task and rushed the papers back to his team. They were irritated that it took him so long, but he was bursting with excitement. He told them about his idea, but no one got excited about his vision. Paul, however, could think of nothing else. He drove to his girlfriend's school two hours away and scouted out sites that might work for his idea.

He found a tiny place that was 100 square feet connected to a hamburger stand. The space rented for $100/month. The front door consisted of a six-foot long wooden flap that swung upwards and hooked like an awning above the storefront. Paul envisioned people coming up to the counter and ordering their copies. He would only need one employee to take the money and run the machine.

He asked a friend of his to paint the front of the building to catch people's attention. Because this was a California college town the artist painted mermaids with faces like Marilyn Monroe all around the opening of the store.

Paul's biggest hurdle was how to gain access to a copier. Xerox rented their machines for $1000/month. He convinced his father to co-sign on a business loan for $5000. Neither his dad nor Harry, the technician who delivered the copy machine to this quirky storefront, thought the business would last very long, especially when he met Paul.

Paul Orfalea was only 22 years old and sported a thick, red afro haircut and walrus mustache. Add to that the bell bottom pants he was wearing and the only thing that kept the technician from thinking he was being pranked was Paul's gracious and confident handshake. When he tells this part of his story he says, "That is why I spend so much time teaching college students about how to present themselves and their ideas. I've found that most ventures in life begin this way," with a confident handshake and the ability to sell an idea.

When it came time to decide on a name for his company, he decided to give it the same name that others had given him based on his thick, kinky hair. Kinkos.

He got his first order even before he was fully ready to open. It was from a professor at the college who needed several copies in a hurry and he paid Paul $50. Gradually the students discovered this tiny place that could help them with their school reports and through word of mouth the profits for Kinkos swelled. Paul's storefront with its humble beginnings became the company that grew into a billion dollar business.

From the very start of the company Paul brought in people to help him. He was still completing his degree in a school two hours away from his startup. He needed someone else to run the copy shop, do his accounting and advise him on the machinery.

He built partnerships and expanded to different regions of California and eventually throughout the United States. From four cents per copy to generating millions of dollars in profit every day, finding a need and fixing it made Paul Orfalea, the man who couldn't read and wouldn't sit still, a billionaire.

Paul attributes his business success to his learning disabilities, which he insists are learning opportunities. Instead of focusing on fixing his own weaknesses, he found ways to fix others' needs.

Not Enough Cookies

Another highly successful business that emerged from discovering a need on campus is Insomnia Cookies. University of Pennsylvania student Seth Berkowitz found that his cravings for something sweet and warm from the oven always hit in the middle of the night when he was studying or conversing with friends. All the on-campus food places were closed and what he really wanted couldn't be retrieved from a vending machine.

Seth began baking cookies in his dorm room when his cravings hit, and he shared samples of the cookies with his friends. He discovered he wasn't the only one with late night munchies. His friends were drawn to the enticing aroma of the brown sugar, cinnamon and chocolate and were willing to pay for the baked goods.

He tested and perfected his recipes by getting feedback from the guys in his residence hall on what they liked best. Everyone began talking about the warm, homemade cookies that you could get at two in the morning and his business expanded.

After college he leased a store front in Syracuse, New York from which he could bake and sell the cookies. College students continued to be his biggest fans, but the word was fast spreading beyond the campus. He discovered that there were people throughout the city who couldn't sleep and needed a fresh baked snack.

He bought a vendor truck and offered warm, fresh cookies by the roadside. As he built his bank account, he added more trucks and finally ventured into the realm of door to door deliveries for cookie hungry patrons.

Today over 100 Insomnia Cookies stores are located throughout the United States. Seth never wondered if he was good enough or smart enough to create a business empire. He just looked for a problem, no matter how small, and found a way to solve it.

Not Enough Eyes

Copies and cookies are obvious needs, especially on college campuses, but the need that Emily Kennedy identified was much more hidden.

While a student at Carnegie Mellon University in Pittsburgh Emily was studying history, ethics and public policy. In her courses she was learning how the internet had inadvertently advanced the criminal business of sex trafficking.

Even as she was taking notes in class, her mind took her back to the haunting moment a few years earlier when she was traveling in Eastern Europe. She was 16 years old and witnessed the harsh reality of children begging on the street. She was told that they were orphans forced by the Russian mob to bring in a certain amount of money each day or they would be beaten.

It was a vivid and disturbing memory for her. She couldn't help but see the similarities to that of women forced into the sex trade here in the United States.

She thought that if the internet was being used to advance this crime there should be a way to use the web to combat it. She chose to do her thesis on human trafficking and interviewed law enforcement officers about their challenges. She was told of their struggles to track how the criminals were advertising their services, where the perpetrators were hiding their bases of operation, and how to find and rescue the victims.

The police knew that Craig's List and Backpage were being used (at that time) to solicit buyers of their victims but they had to page through the ads individually. It took hours of time to piece together a picture of the culprit's operation and by the time they identified a pattern the perpetrators had changed their locations and web addresses. It was extremely time consuming and they did not have enough people to devote to tracking the criminal activity.

The problem was bigger than she realized and daunting to the law enforcement community, but she kept digging for solutions. Emily says, "I heard that people [involved in this crime] were traveling across cities and states, or that they would change their phone numbers over time. But there was no data out there to show it. I thought, 'How cool would it be if you could use online data to track and rescue victims?'"

Emily's specialty was in research. She knew how to interpret data. She just had to find a way that she could use artificial intelligence to collect and track the data that was needed. A computer could accomplish the work of thousands of people and at a much faster rate.

Emily was not a computer science major. She knew she did not have the technical skills to pursue her idea. Instead of giving up in frustration, Emily, like Paul Orfalea, sought out people who had the skills she lacked. She went to the Auton Lab at the university's Robotics Institute to ask some questions. She wasn't even sure what questions to ask. All she had was an idea.

Dr. Artur Dubrawski, the director of the lab was intrigued by her passion and focus. He introduced her to researchers and computer programmers, some of whom caught her vision and were eager to help. Together they created the programs that generated the data Emily needed to track and flag the online activities that indicated the behavior of sex traffickers.

In 2013 her program, Traffic Jam, was launched. It was the first suite of artificial intelligence tools under the business name of Marinus Analytics that would prove valuable in rescuing victims and arresting the perpetrators. Convincing law enforcement to use it, however, was slower in coming.

At the beginning of her business, Emily had some very high hurdles to overcome. It was hard to get people to take her seriously. She was young, a 22-year-old woman in a male dominated field who was looking to transform the way that law enforcement had always tackled this problem. However, as they began to see the value of her system, they were able to use it to shut down sex trafficking operations that had thwarted their efforts for years. The light began to rise on Marinus Analytics.

Through her leadership abilities she has been able to convince world class researchers, programmers and FBI agents to get on board with her vision. The software has continued to be developed and now includes a facial recognition element. "When we released it there was a detective who had been trying to [find and rescue] an underage individual for weeks, by looking at online social media activity," Cara Jones, co-founder and CEO of Marinus Analytics says. "We found her whereabouts in seconds."

Emily's research and development company deals with a very dark subject, yet she remains positive and dedicated. When asked how she does it she replied, "I remember thinking when I was a researcher, 'If all this work gives one person the chance to get out of a life of exploitation, then all of that work is worth it.'

15

Divergent Thinking

*"If you always do what you always did, you will
always get what you always got."*
— Albert Einstein

The art museum was packed. People were lined up
throughout the building and standing still, almost like
stone statues themselves. Since I had volunteered to help
ensure that things went smoothly at this gala event, I
searched to see who was holding up the line. I discovered a
small bent-over man at the front. He was holding a cane
under one arm and slowly gliding his gnarled hands over
the muscled sculpture of a bronze cougar crouched on a
boulder. There were tears rolling down his face.

I had never before seen one person so moved by
examining an artist's work. He spent nearly 30 minutes at
this one piece of art, but no one behind him seemed to
mind. Each person in the line behind him was equally
pensive, quiet and unhurried. In fact, when the man
moved to the next sculpture the woman behind him was
hesitant to move forward because she was entranced by

the artwork she was deciphering with her fingers. It was the most unusual experience I had ever witnessed.

Tom and I were newly married, and he was the Communications Director for the Museum of Touch in Atlanta, Georgia. Tom had helped launch this museum where guests were not only *allowed* to touch everything, they were *encouraged* to do so. It was the first of its kind for an art museum. The guest list at this gala was reserved for the community of persons who were visually impaired.

The art lovers who attended the event were guided to one sculpture after another and encouraged to touch and "see" every nuance of the pieces. Some could barely contain the emotion that flooded their whole being. These guests had never been allowed to explore artwork in this way. It was extremely moving.

Many students come to college blind as well. By that I mean they cannot see the opportunities in front of them. They are given a college advisor who is assigned anywhere from 400 to 1,000 students to work with. The advice they give is to direct the student from enrollment to graduation. They don't have time to give any more insight into college success than that.

The most successful students step out of their comfort zones and explore what they cannot readily see. They ask themselves, "What if?" What if I saw from a different perspective, through someone else's eyes? What if I did things differently than what has always been done before?"

Zach

Zach Winkler came to college with a singular focus. He always knew that he wanted to pursue a career in technology because he loved computers and working with technology came easily to him. Before he even graduated from high school he was creating and selling apps through the Apple store. This was his hobby and his delight, and he wanted to make it his career.

He has a very playful spirit and a heart that cares about people. At the University of Missouri Zach found other students who loved technology as much as he did and they became fast friends. He declared his major in computer science and continued to tinker with creating gaming apps.

He would have been happy doing just that while completing his degree and hanging out with friends. However, one day he opened an email that he says entirely changed the trajectory of his life.

It was a bulk email containing an invitation to attend a meeting. Some students in the journalism department needed help from students in the computer science department to create an app for a competition.

Zach was very candid when he told Tom and me that he had no interest in a journalism project and no intention of going to that informational meeting. He didn't know anyone in that major, but his curiosity tugged at him to just go and check it out. Besides, he liked to help people.

At the meeting he heard what the students were trying to do, and how they were desperate for the kind of expertise he had to make their ideas actually work. Zach was impressed by the journalism students with whom he spoke and intrigued by their concepts. He agreed to partner with them to build the app they had in mind.

Together the team worked for three months on the project, trying and perfecting the app. Zach said it really stretched him intellectually. Although he had created many successful gaming apps in the past this was the first app that would have a practical application.

By seeing through the eyes of journalists and learning what they needed he was able to create something that could revolutionize their jobs. The app gave journalists the ability to quickly pair a news story with ads that would be of interest to the readers of that story. The team submitted the app to the Reynolds Journalism Institute Tech Competition and won first place!

That was just the fire Zach needed. His mind exploded with creative ideas, thinking of ways he could solve problems using apps. He got to work on another project, but it failed. So, he started on the next idea, but it failed miserably as well. "Each attempt," he said, "was a good accident that stretched my thinking even further. I just wanted to try more ideas."

One day at lunch he was talking with some of his friends who were in the nursing program. The nursing students told him they were required to do an internship at the nearby hospital. Often the students would return to campus at three in the morning and it made them feel very vulnerable walking in from the dark parking lot alone.

The college was aware of this problem and to ensure safety for the students they installed blue poles throughout the campus that had a button to call campus police. Students were instructed that when they felt threatened, they could push the button and wait for the campus police to arrive who would escort them back to the residence hall.

Some of Zach's women friends complained that they did not feel safe standing at the pole waiting for help. If they were being stalked, they preferred to run to safety. They needed a portable panic button that would travel with them. This got him to thinking, "Perhaps I can make an app for that."

He set to work on this new idea and within a week he had created the first version of his "hold until safe" app. He called it SafeTrek (updated in 2018 to NoonLight). The concept was that the person who felt they were in a dangerous situation could hold down a button on their phone until they were in a safe place. When they reached safety, the person would let go of the button and enter in their four-digit code to signal that they no longer needed help. If, however, they let go of the button and did not punch in the code, police would be immediately notified to go and help the person.

The app functions similarly to making a 911 call without having to make the call, only better. When someone dials 911 from a cell phone the emergency services cannot find the exact location of the caller. The 911 equipment was built to identify the home address of a phone call, not the actual location of a cell phone in real time. The caller must be able to explain to the emergency operator where they are standing and they may not know. Other times the caller may not want to speak out loud because they are hiding from a threatening individual.

Listening to his women friends' concerns, Zach understood their feelings of vulnerability and knew he could solve that problem. The NoonLight app that he built utilizes the cell phone's GPS capability so that it pinpoints the user's location for police. This app won another award at the RJI Tech Competition, but it was far from everything that Zach wanted it to be.

Zach and his business partner Aaron Kunnemann, whom he met in college, continued to work tirelessly to expand the capabilities of the app. Their initial vision was to make a safety tool for college students, but it is now so much more than that. They have expanded to 70 call centers where calls are monitored and information is relayed to the police. They have created maps that can show city councilmen the locations where people feel most unsafe.

NoonLight has contracted with Amazon's Alexa so that the user can say, "Alexa, tell NoonLight to send help." It also works with other devices like Nest Protect and Ring to protect one's home. They have even made it compatible to work with health apps like FitBit to notify emergency services if, for example, the user's heart rate indicates a heart attack.

With over two million subscribers the business is a phenomenal success, but Zach recalls the first time that what he was doing became "real" for him. He tells the story of when a young woman triggered the help button on her phone. The business was very new with only a few subscribers and only one call center.

Zach was working the call center alone and he called her back to see if she did indeed need help. Someone picked up the phone and hung it up again. He heard laughter in the background. He texted her with the same question, "Do you need help?" A text came back telling him, "That b**** is dead!"

Zach contacted the police in the girl's area and told them where she was when the first trigger came through. He told them that he was tracking the movement of her cell phone on the dashboard he had built. He told the police to look for one or more girls running west on a particular street from the point of first contact.

The police were amazed that Zach was able to give them such detailed information and with his assistance they located the victim. She had been severely beaten and needed medical help right away. The police also found and arrested the perpetrators who still held the girl's phone.

Zach was a recent graduate from college when this incident occurred and he still gets emotional when he talks about it. His technology was less than six months old. He and his business partner were taking turns running the 24/7 call center while both of them worked full time jobs elsewhere to pay the bills. He wasn't sure the two of them could keep up this pace. However, when the mother of the young woman called to thank him for saving her daughter's life, he knew the app was something he could stake his life on and the lives of many others as well.

Zack said, "I wish I would have spent more of my free time [in college] building products and trying to launch company ideas with other students. The second you start your first job, the ability to take that amount of risk becomes extremely difficult and to get that amount of experience in the real world could take decades."

Tom and I encourage you to think "outside of the box" while in college. Make friends with those in different majors and share your ideas. Be creative! Perhaps an idea you develop with others can change the world, save a life or become a career.

16

The Force Awakens: Passion to Purpose

"There is no passion to be found in playing small – in settling
for a life that is less than the one you are capable of living."
— Nelson Mandela

Michael Skinner was a student with big ideas. He was
studying to be a mechanical engineer at the University of
Notre Dame, but he didn't just want a degree, he wanted
to make a difference in the world. He joined a campus club
that was started in 2016 called e-NABLE. There he met the
president of the club, Cole Grabowski and other
engineering students who, like him, had a passion to do
something with their lives that mattered.

The e-NABLE club was given access to the 3D printing
technology on campus and the students were eager to use
it for a worthy cause. They had created small plastic toys
and other fun gadgets, but they hungered to do more with
the technology.

Perhaps it was because of the many thoughts Michael had whirling around in his head, or maybe he just missed the email that detailed what he was required to wear. Whatever the reason, he showed up in the wrong attire at a college event to honor the parents.

He had to do some quick thinking to rectify this little dilemma. Michael called for an Uber driver to pick him up and take him to his residence so that he could change into something more appropriate than jeans and a T-shirt.

It was inconvenient for him and a little embarrassing because he knew his friends would ask him why he was late to the event, but Michael made the most of the time by chatting with the Uber driver, Doug Anderson. They conversed easily and when Michael asked Doug about his family, Doug was only too eager to share anecdotes about the joys of his life, his adopted children.

As they talked Doug casually mentioned that Tori, his 11-year old daughter, was born with only one digit on each hand. If the seat belt had not been holding him down Michael would have jumped out of his seat! Doug's daughter was the perfect client for the e-NABLE team. They could create functioning 3D printed hands for her.

One prosthetic hand typically costs over $10,000 and Tori needed two. Even if the family could afford the prosthetics it is not recommended to purchase one for a child as they are continually outgrowing them. However, the e-NABLE team could make her inexpensive 3D printed hands that could be readily replaced as she grew into adulthood.

Tori was eager to be the recipient of the project. She was involved every step along the way. The engineering students measured her hands and adapted the patterns. They learned their skills by doing and they created customized patterns for each hand that would fit around her one digit. Tori asked that her hands be made of purple and blue plastic. She told them that these were the colors that make her smile.

The team created two customized robotic hands that, as Cole described them, are "wrist-driven, which means that Tori is able to close the fingers in the hand by flexing her wrist." For the first time she would be able to have functioning fingers with the capability to pick up and throw a softball or hold a glass in one hand. Working with these robotic hands would prepare her for an actual prosthetic when she was older.

That serendipitous meeting in an Uber on a mission to get a tie brought a bond of friendship between the engineering students at Notre Dame and a family in need. Cole said, "I hope to continue to work with a lot of great kids like Tori."

Doug says, "God made it all line up like that, that's no coincidence for me."

A Tale of Two Brothers

Christopher and Michael are fraternal twins. They were born to a Catholic couple in Iowa. Christopher was a healthy ten and a half pounds at birth while his tiny brother struggled with many physical challenges weighing in at only four pounds. They nearly lost Michael on the day of his birth, but through the tireless work of doctors and nurses both boys survived, and their parents loved them dearly.

As the boys grew, they became best friends. Each wanted to do what the other was doing. They played together, laughed together and always sat side by side. However, as they grew their difference in abilities threatened to separate them. Michael lagged further and further behind Christopher in development. He couldn't run alongside his brother. He couldn't play basketball at even close to the level of Christopher.

When their parents questioned doctors as to what was wrong with Michael, the twins' parents learned that he had a mild form of cerebral palsy. He had trouble walking and using the right side of his body. He was nearly deaf in one ear and needed strong corrective lenses to see clearly.

Christopher, on the other hand, was developing normally and seemed to have inherited all the advantages that his brother lacked.

At 13 years of age they almost lost Michael again. His heart stopped. His parents were told they needed to either tell him their last goodbyes or agree to let the doctors try a pump that would prolong his life for a mere 48 hours. Their only hope would be for him to receive a heart transplant. They chose to opt for the pump and pray and wait. Miraculously, a donor heart arrived 24 hours later!

Michael successful received the new heart but was told that the heart would probably last only about seven years. Throughout the whole hospital ordeal Christopher could not be removed from his brother's side.

Even with the new heart, Michael's challenges continued to be a heavy burden on the family both financially and emotionally. The stress exacerbated a rift between their parents and when the twins turned 16 their parents parted ways. This hit the boys hard.

Both boys were exceptionally intelligent and thrived in the school environment but there was an anger that rose up inside Christopher because he was not able to fix what was broken, neither his parents' relationship nor his brother's physical challenges. Christopher struggled with guilt over his own good health and for the abilities that came easily to him. He agonized for his brother. Nothing came easily for Michael.

With all the heartache at home Christopher found welcome solace in the drama department, spending long hours after school rehearsing and performing in the high school plays. He made plans to go to college and study biochemical engineering in hopes that he could find a cure for his brother's heart ailment. His high grades were setting him up for well-paying scholarships, but his internal anxieties erupted in external acting out that nearly derailed his future.

In his senior year Christopher, with the assistance of his cousin, broke into their high school at midnight with the intent of stealing some money. He was caught and convicted of third-degree burglary.

He was sentenced to three years' probation and 180 hours of community service. It also cost him his reputation in his home town and the anticipated scholarships evaporated. Christopher, however, credits the incident with "straightening him out."

Christopher enrolled at the University of Iowa. His brother Michael went to Mount Mercy University in Cedar Rapids. Christopher's acting out continued. At college he was surrounded by young people ready to party and he was the heartiest of partiers. He said that he often awoke not even aware of where he had been the night before because of his excessive drinking.

Although he was tested and confirmed to have an IQ of 160 - the same as Stephen Hawking - his grades, his choices and behavior were not reflecting that intelligence. His brother Michael, in the meantime, was making wise choices and doing well in his courses.

The University of Iowa had an enrollment of nearly 20,000 undergraduate students and was a great place for talent scouts to search for and recruit young people. At 6' 2" with an athletic build and masculine features, Christopher attracted attention wherever he went.

A recruiter heard the laughter and spotted Christopher at the center of a group of college students leading the fun as usual. The recruiter waited until the crowd thinned out and approached him. He asked him if he could interest him in entering a modeling competition. It could lead to significant prize money if he won.

It had been difficult for the family to come up with the money for college tuition, so Christopher decided to enter his name and photo into "Fresh Faces of Iowa." His good looks and talent combined to earn him first place.

One part of the prize package was a trip to New York City for the International Modeling and Talent Association (IMTA) Convention. Here he was able to participate in talent competitions and meet with talent agents from across the country. He was well received and became convinced that his future was in acting. He dropped out of college and moved to Los Angeles.

His brother Michael wished Christopher the best of luck and continued with his education. He graduated from Mount Mercy University with a business degree and a minor in finance.

Michael became a successful salesman, but what brought him the most joy in his life was speaking and fundraising for various non-profits like Reaching for the Stars, A Foundation of Hope for Children with Cerebral Palsy like himself. Happily, the heart he was given at age thirteen that was only predicted to last seven years has continued to serve him well nearly 30 years later.

As for Christopher, the acting career worked out pretty well for him. He became the face of Calvin Klein products in 1997 and in 1998 landed a recurring role in *That 70s Show*. His career as an actor was launched.

College did not result in a degree in biochemical engineering as he had planned. He will not be the one to discover a cure for his brother's heart ailment. Instead, college placed him in the right place at the right time to meet the talent scout who pointed him in a new direction.

Christopher has earned millions of dollars through his acting. With that income he has earned significantly more through wise investing. Some of his very successful investments were with Uber, Skype, and Airbnb, recognizing their potential when they were just start-ups.

Christopher continued learning and stretching himself beyond acting and beyond investing. In 2013 he even worked as a product engineer at Lenovo to help create the Yoga Tablet 2 Pro. However, like his brother Michael, what he loves the most is helping people.

He has supported numerous charities and even started one of his own. He is a co-founder of the non-profit, Thorn, that with a team of brilliant developers works to put an end to the spread of child sexual abuse. Hundreds of children have been rescued from child traffickers through their work.

He has known the ache of wanting to ease the pain for others and today, because of his wealth he is able to do just that. The world knows him better by his middle name, Christopher **Ashton** Kutcher.

Ashton summed up his life philosophy when he was asked to tell the best investment that he ever made. Quietly he replied, "My relationships."

17

Be Good for Nothing

"Volunteering is the ultimate exercise in democracy. You vote in elections once a year, but when you volunteer, you vote every day about the kind of community you want to live in".
— Author Unknown

I felt like Cinderella in the Prince's ballroom. When I read the invitation to the end-of-year gala I was determined to attend. I had never been to a gala before. I asked my friends for help and was given a formal gown that I could borrow.

Wide-eyed with excitement, I walked into the ballroom clutching my purse that contained the invitation. I didn't know what to expect. There was a quartet playing music and the round tables were expertly decorated with beautiful floral arrangements. There were cloth napkins folded in the shape of flowers and nestled on each plate.

"I received an invitation," I said timidly to the greeter who asked for my name. He nodded and smiled warmly. After checking his list of attendees, he seated me near the front of the room. I didn't personally know anyone there, but I recognized the mayor of the city. I gazed down at my plate to keep from meeting anyone's eyes. I was afraid someone would notice that I was just a college kid and ask me to leave.

I startled when a waiter reached in front of me, took my napkin, shook it open and laid it on my lap. Then the food was brought out one course at a time and every plate was amazing. Midway through the meal another waiter poured me a glass of champagne and the host asked everyone to raise their glasses in a toast to celebrate a fantastic year. I smiled and raised my glass. I was finally beginning to relax, and then my name was called. I was asked to stand.

How had I gotten here, I wondered? I thought back to the project I had initiated on campus. I wanted to do something to make a difference, to raise money for a cause that I cared about. I also wanted it to be fun. I gathered some friends from my residence hall and came up with the idea of holding a Dance for Those Who Can't to raise money for the Muscular Dystrophy Association.

I approached the administration at the University of Tulsa to ask them about using the gym. They gave me some paperwork to fill out and I followed through with the process of getting the approval. My friends and I created a music play list, printed up posters and created decorations.

The idea was for the students to come and have fun, but to get in they would have to make a cash donation to MDA. The plan worked! Students came, students donated, and students danced. Afterwards, I gathered the donations and brought them to the MDA offices in Tulsa. It was a significant donation of a little over $1,000, but was paltry compared to what I had hoped to raise.

Now, a few months later I stood to be honored at the gala. The president of the MDA chapter in Tulsa explained what I had done at my college to raise money for the association. Then she asked for applause and I blushed.

The rest of that evening community leaders and business executives, some dressed in tuxedoes, introduced themselves to me and asked about my future plans. Again and again I was told that the kind of initiative I showed is unusual in young people. "If you ever need a job, give me a call."

I came away from that event with a stack of business cards from some very important people. I had volunteered to make a difference in the world, but unexpectedly, it had opened up the world to me.

Veterinarian to Leadership Trainer

Everyone knew Julie Marie Carrier would become a veterinarian. Whenever she met a stranger who was walking their dog, she would kneel to welcome their pet and pat its head. If she was visiting a friend who had a pet, she could pat her lap and their cat would nuzzle into her arms. She was often told, "My cat doesn't come to anyone. How did you get her to jump up on your lap?"

Julie loved animals and she had the peaceful demeanor that animals trusted. To be a vet where she would work with animals every day seemed to be the natural choice.

Julie enrolled at Ohio State University and immersed herself in the courses she would need to be accepted into veterinary school once her bachelor's degree was completed. She took biology, anatomy, and chemistry. Her classes were filled with students who were planning to go on to medical school. To become a veterinarian her education requirements would also take eight years to complete, just like any other doctor.

She was in her senior year when she realized she did not enjoy her classes. She hadn't for a long time. She needed to be focused on applying to post-graduate veterinary schools and her heart just wasn't in it.

"What's wrong with me?" she wondered. "Becoming a vet is what I've always thought I should do, but what if it's not what I want to do?"

For her senior year Julie studied abroad in Manchester, England on a Rotary Ambassadorial Scholarship. It was a fabulous opportunity and she enjoyed the new experience, but she was not happy. The discouraging thought hit her, "I have no idea what I should do with my life, but I know I don't want to be a vet." Since she was far away from family and friends, she had some time to scrutinize her life without having to answer any well-meaning questions.

Julie did the same kind of exercise that our *College Superhero Secrets* training program leads students through to find their ideal career paths. She started by listing the things that she had done in the past that might give her a clue as to what she would enjoy as a career.

She wrote down what she was good at doing naturally (her talents), and what she loved doing. Where these activities overlapped, she would find her ideal career. She circled the activities that made her the happiest, along with any classes that she particularly enjoyed and a pattern began to emerge.

Julie remembered that she flourished during the times when she volunteered for the youth leadership conferences. She enjoyed working with young people and helping them recognize their own worth. It was demanding work with no pay, but because it was so rewarding, she would have done it every day if she could.

She also noticed that her favorite classes at Ohio State had been the communication and leadership courses. There was the overlap. Encouraged by this revelation she chose to take courses in communication and media performance while she was in England.

Upon returning to Ohio State she had a dilemma. She wanted to change her major to leadership studies, but the college had no such program. Being a woman of small stature but strong conviction, Julie approached the administration about the idea of creating her own program.

After much research and several meetings, the college opened a new program, her program of leadership studies. The requirements were very different than that of her previous major and added two additional years to her degree completion, but she was thrilled that she could pursue what made her happy.

Fueled by the knowledge of her purpose Julie pushed forward with a dedication that she had never known before. After graduation she was hired at the Pentagon in a senior management position of leadership and training.

With her focus on leadership she pursued and won the Miss Virginia USA competition. This title gave her national visibility and fame and enabled her to launch a leadership program for kids nationwide.

She continues to inspire and educate young people through her nationwide speaking tours and as a confidence coach on MTV's *MADE*. Julie went to college to become a veterinarian. Instead, she found her passion and purpose as a result of volunteering.

All students, whether they know exactly what they want to pursue in the way of a career or if they are still trying to figure things out can benefit greatly from volunteering. It gives the student the opportunity to look behind the curtain of different professions. The student builds friendships, not only with other students, but with adults in the business world, cultivating lucrative connections and, most importantly, the student can get some valuable experience.

I often hear college graduates complain that they cannot get a job because the employer wants both education and job experience. One student told me, "The jobs I want require a degree and three years of experience. How do they expect a college graduate to have three years of job experience? I have been busy getting my degree!" Volunteering during summers, spring breaks, or even during the school year can help solve that dilemma.

Hero for a Day

One afternoon when Aubrey Blankenship, a communications major at Grand Canyon University, was volunteering at a nearby elementary school she experienced an emergency lockdown. Six-year-old Miguel scooted over to sit closer to her as the kids and teachers hunkered down in the hallway. His eyes darted about in fear. There was a gunman in the neighborhood who had already shot someone.

The kids could not leave the school until the police caught the perpetrator and gave the school administrators the assurance that it was safe to leave. They had to sit in the hallway where they were safer than in the classroom that had windows.

"I want to go home," Miguel sniffled, trying to be brave. Aubrey smiled and reassured him that the lockdown would be over soon. She opened *The Cat in the Hat* storybook and urged him to sound out the words. Other first graders joined their little group. She did her best to distract the kids from the drama at hand and to help the time go faster as they waited.

Aubrey enjoyed being a reading assistant for the kids at this elementary school in an impoverished area. She volunteered two afternoons each week. She told me, "Even though I had no desire to be a teacher, the time I spent with the kids gave me a chance to get off campus and focus on their needs rather than my own. It helped me keep my perspective on what was important."

Although she had plenty of other responsibilities including writing and editing articles for the college newspaper and working two part-time jobs, the volunteer tutoring gave her a chance to be a hero to these kids and had the added benefit of reducing her own stress. The day of the lockdown she comforted the children and got to witness their joy when the school told them the crisis was over and they could all go home. She felt she had done something that truly mattered.

Social Capital

Froswa' (fros-wah) Booker-Drew, PhD is a firm believer in building "social capital." This is the phrase she uses for building meaningful relationships. She also believes that the best way to do that is through volunteerism. "Relationships are critical to one's success," she told me and then she explained her own experience.

When she was in her undergrad studies, she was focused on becoming an attorney, but the longer she pursued that path the more she felt that it was not a good fit for her. She wanted to help people and found that she could do it in a different way that better fit her personality.

Froswa' told me that her first job came about as a result of her volunteering on a project. She said, "I had no idea that the adults were watching my work and decided to offer me a job. My first boss, Michele Bobadilla, is still my mentor more than 25 years later!" Froswa' insists that being intentional about building relationships is the way to succeed in any field and volunteering is a perfect way to build relationships.

Froswa' is the former Diversity Ambassador for the Red Cross, a volunteer position. She has presented workshops at the United Nations. She is the former National Community Engagement Director for World Vision and is currently a coach, a trainer and the Director of Community Affairs for the State Fair of Texas. She is also the author of *Rules of Engagement: Making Connections Last*. By all accounts she is a highly successful person, but it all started by connecting with just one person as a volunteer.

Resume Filler

Robert Christianson, an aerospace engineering major at Arizona State University found volunteering to be a great way to fill out his resume and gain some experience. He said, "When you're trying to get your first job, anything helps. These volunteering opportunities are what you should put in lieu of work experience. Networking is conceptually simple, but difficult to go out and do. Volunteering gives you an authentic means to meet people and impress them with what you're made of."

Through volunteering to raise money for MDA I inadvertently discovered a way to stand out and be noticed by potential employers. Julie Marie Carrier was able to experience the thrill of impacting the lives of young people through her volunteering and discovered her passion. Aubrey Blankenship used it to keep her perspective at a time when many of her peers were drowning in personal frustration and overwhelm. Dr. Froswa' Booker-Drew landed her first job and gained a valuable mentor. Robert Christianson was able to put himself ahead of the crowd by populating his resume with genuine work experience.

It is interesting to note that based on national surveys, 75% of college students in 2018 stated that they believe it is essential that everyone do something to help others who are struggling, but fewer students than ever are actually volunteering their time to do good and those numbers continue to decline. For anyone willing to jump into the pool of volunteerism this is great news. That student who does good for no payment will be one of the few who is recognized for having the initiative that is valuable to employers.

Robert is proof of this. "Since this is my freshman year of college, my prospects for internships were remarkably low," Christianson said. "I had read that most engineering freshmen had to submit at least 250 applications to even have a chance of getting a few interviews, let alone a job. I submitted 31 applications; I got two interviews. Volunteering activities helped me because not many applicants typically have that volume of project and leadership experience."

Why volunteer?

- Less depression issues
- Increase self-esteem and happiness
- Lower stress
- Develop new friendships
- Build professional relationships
- Cultivate lucrative references
- Achieve career goals
- Helps you stand out
- Like the Grinch, you grow your heart

How it helps:

- Employers love hiring kind and altruistic people – sets you apart
- Volunteer hours count as work experience to most employers
- Keeping track of specific actions and what came out of what you did can make you more attractive to employers looking for those experiences
- Every volunteer job is a compilation of many skills. You can highlight different ones to match different job interviews
- Chance to network- get to know the staff and executive director. Some of the most powerful people in the community sit on the boards of non-profits
- Change someone else's life and grow as a leader
- Refine and define your skills

18

Don't Always Believe the Professor

*"Think for yourself or others will think for you
without thinking of you."*
— Henry David Thoreau

When I first met Diane Dresback she was scrutinizing a scene through the eye of an enormous camera. Stretching up on her tiptoes to get a better angle she looked like a child, but there was no mistaking that she was assisting the director. She had written the screenplay and she knew what it should look like on screen.

On the floor in front of her was the shattered glass that the actress Katherine Stewart had intentionally knocked off the counter. It was a critical moment in the movie *Atrophy* (originally titled *Paranoia*) for which Diane later won the 2012 Arizona Filmmaker of the Year Award.

Diane pointed to a part of the background that needed to be included in the scene. The cameraman nodded his understanding and adjusted the camera as the actors awaited the signal that they were back "on." She directed like a conductor before an orchestra, making sure all the elements played together in harmony.

Diane is not only a talented movie maker, but also a screenwriter and author as well. I had to know how she got started and if college was the catalyst to her success. She said that yes, it was, but not in the way I might expect.

In college she was studying business. To make ends meet she worked off campus throughout her undergrad program. She told me, "I am a big advocate of people working while in college. It helps them to determine what they want to do and more importantly, what they don't want to do when they get out."

Her four-year education stretched into six years because she changed her major several times. She said that she had picked business, thinking that was the practical major to have, but she found herself dreading her classes and not doing very well academically. She had tried other majors but could not settle on a satisfactory direction.

Finally, she was encouraged to visit the Career Counseling Office. The career assessment test she was given indicated that she was a people person. She changed her major one last time to human services with an emphasis in social work and counseling. This major included classes in psychology and sociology, knowledge that she has found to be useful throughout her life. She loved this focus and her grades began to improve.

Diane remembered that she enjoyed writing stories in her childhood and teen years and had always gotten good grades on her efforts. She chose to enroll in a creative writing course to satisfy one of her core requirements. She couldn't wait to get started.

"So, did that course begin your writing and filmmaking endeavors?" I asked.

Diane responded, "Oh no. Quite the contrary." She then told me about the day that the professor stood in front of the entire class and read her short story out loud. He verbally tore it to shreds. Diane could feel the blood rush to her face as she felt the sting of humiliation. Later in his office the professor told her, "You aren't good enough to write. Don't pursue it as a profession."

Diane said, "I believed him. So, I quit writing."

She says the professor was probably just trying to help her. It was not said in a malicious way, but it tore a hole in her soul. Diane graduated and went on to get her master's degree while raising a family and working full time. She had many successful years working in Human Resources for large companies, writing for business and training purposes, but still she did not write creatively.

When her oldest son Trenton was 16 years old, she told him about a story she desperately wanted to put down on paper but wasn't sure that she could. Trenton had seen his petite mom, who he now towered over, conquer many difficult situations so he urged her to just do it. What was the problem?

Diane explained to him what had happened in that classroom more than twenty years earlier. The professor's words repeated in her head every time she attempted to write. With the bluntness and outspoken wisdom of a teenager Trenton said, "Mom, you're letting this professor have too much control over you!" Those words broke a crack in her wall of insecurities and she began to allow herself to start building stories in her mind.

It took her three years from that conversation with her son to take her first step putting her stories onto paper. She wrote a screenplay but felt it was terrible, so she studied books on creative writing. She also sought out and attended workshops, expanding her knowledge and practicing her craft.

Diane's courage continued to grow and she took on more creative projects. She joined 48-hour film challenges, working with teams to create movies on a short time limit. She co-wrote, directed, and even acted in some of the films, culminating in her becoming the 2012 Arizona Filmmaker of the Year for her movie, *Atrophy*.

In 2014 she wrote *Promise of Protection,* her first novel, and shook off the rest of her professor's negative influence. In rapid succession she wrote three more novels, *Reminisce*, *Postponement* and *Room for Another*. Each of her novels are highly visual, conjuring up images in the reader's minds as though they are ripe for movie production.

I asked her, "So, how did college help you do what you're doing now?" She said that she uses the knowledge she gained from the psychology and sociology courses to write greater depth into her fictional characters.

She even values her experience with the negative writing professor. It gave her an understanding of how just a few words can block a person from fulfilling their potential. She has been able to draw from that experience when writing characters for both her films and novels and give them rich backstories that she could not have done any other way.

I have watched Diane in action with the teams she assembles to create movies. She knows how to motivate and inspire her people, the exact opposite of what her professor did with her.

The Dr. of Dinosaurs

The dinosaurs of *Jurassic Park* thundered into the lives of millions of Americans, letting us experience the fear and chaos that would ensue if we had biologically regenerated dinosaurs to roam about in the modern day. Michael Crichton is the author of that book and 27 more novels, 16 of which were compelling enough to be made into movies.

However, like Dresback, Crichton was also discouraged from pursuing writing by his college professor who persisted in giving him significantly low marks on his papers. Frustrated, Crichton was certain that his work was being unfairly graded.

To confirm his suspicions, he confided in another professor that he was going to try an experiment. He copied an essay that was originally written by renowned author George Orwell and submitted it in his own name. The grade came back as a B-.

Although he had his proof that the professor was not grading him fairly, he was discouraged. It was hard enough to be battling against his professor, but as he told it on the Official Website of Michael Crichton, "I read that only two hundred writers in America support themselves writing. I thought, that's an awfully small group." He decided to become a medical doctor instead.

His passion for writing did not go away, however. He paid his way through college by writing thrillers under a couple of different pseudonyms even while studying medicine and sold them to major publishers.

He graduated with his MD from Harvard Medical school, but he never became a practicing doctor. Shortly before his graduation the movie rights for his novel, *The Andromeda Strain* were sold. Both the movie and his book became wildly popular. As a result, he hung up his stethoscope and became laser-focused on his career as a writer.

Although he was dissuaded from pursuing his original intent of getting a degree in English, his studies in anthropology, biology and medicine fed his creative mind with a depth of material that spawned his bestselling science fiction books. From the biogenetically created Tyrannosaur Rex of *Jurassic Park* to the terrifying virus from outer space that threatened to wipe out all mankind that he called the *Andromeda Strain,* he ended up where he had always wanted to go. The world is richer because he didn't listen to his professor.

The Illustrator

There are many stories of college professors who have dished out discouragement. Fortunately, there are also many excellent professors who inspire their students to rise above their own limitations. You will learn later in this book about a professor who was instrumental in the success of Warren Buffett, helping him to rise to the pinnacle of the financial world. This professor continued to act as a mentor throughout Buffett's life.

However, there are also professors who, for whatever reason, lose sight of their mission to motivate students to reach and exceed their goals. They are either unwilling to take the time they should with a student or they make a quick judgement about the student's potential. The professor sees just a snapshot of where the student is at that moment and believes it is locked in time, as though there will be no growth or development.

When I was in college, my goal was to be an illustrator. I envisioned children's books with brightly colored pictures and magazines with my artwork emblazoned on the covers stacked on coffee tables throughout the country. To this intent I studied graphic design and drawing, painting and commercial art. I had amazing professors at the University of Tulsa and felt I was growing in my abilities. I worked each summer at my dad's design studio getting practical experience and I brought that knowledge to my assignments at the college.

Brad Place, the Chairman of the College of Arts at TU was very approachable and discussed with me my future career plans. In my sophomore year when I was discouraged and wanted to drop out of school just for a semester or two, we sat and talked again.

He told me that the second year of college is the most volatile time when students who choose to drop out typically do. This is because the student is still stuck completing core and prerequisite courses and is not yet able to take the courses they really want for their major. It is also difficult to see the end goal when the student is not yet even halfway through their four-year journey.

I insisted that it would just be for a break, but he said when students leave, they get involved in a job and the majority of the time do not ever return to complete their degrees. Brad picked up the phone and said, "Let me give your dad a quick call and see what he thinks about this." He acted like he had him on speed dial. I panicked. I hadn't told my dad anything about my plans to leave school!

"Don't do that!" I pleaded, "I'll talk to him about it later." But I never did. I stayed in college. I wanted my degree and just having someone talk me through my decision helped me solidify my intent to complete what I started.

It wasn't until years later that I realized Brad Place couldn't have had my dad on speed dial, but he sure convinced me at the time. It was no wonder that his daughter Mary Kay Place became an Emmy Award winning actor! The talent was in her genes.

That was the good side of college, but the one professor that nearly stopped me in my tracks came into my life my senior year. I had been doing well in my classes and enjoying the assignments, but one afternoon my professor of illustration walked over and stood by my art table. He said, "Realize you will never be an illustrator. Very few ever make it." He told me how he had attempted to break into the field himself but was not able to do it.

I was stunned by his words. Here was a guy whose artwork I admired. I was learning from him and yet he was saying the career was not possible. Being an illustrator of books and magazines was all I had ever aspired to do and I was about to graduate.

I fretted over his proclamation and became disheartened, but after a week or two I got angry. The more I thought about what he had said, the more I rejected it. He could not foresee my future and he had no control over it! His words became a rallying cry for me to prove him wrong.

When I graduated, I had two different design studios offer me a job. I supported myself as a graphic designer for a few years. I was designing logos and creating layouts for brochures, but I still wanted to break into illustration.

I decided to leave the design studio and launch my own company. I presented my portfolio to various art directors and was hired to create over 500 professional illustrations. I had the joy of seeing my artwork published in Chicago Magazine, OK Magazine, Georgia Magazine and Ford Times. My artwork was being seen in thousands of homes on album covers, posters and in books. I had done what my professor had claimed was impossible.

I took a long hiatus from studio work to raise four children and then, because of my passion to help students, I transitioned into college advising, but the desire to be creative kept nagging at me. My husband Tom encouraged me to get back into my artwork as a hobby.

While gazing upon some of my watercolors one day he said, "What if we turned these into greeting cards?" On that simple idea we founded Peaks Publishing Inc as a side business just to bring in enough money to cover a monthly car payment. That would be the deciding factor as to whether or not we would continue this little side venture.

I painted watercolor images and Tom designed the cards, had them printed and packaged for sale. The first card we released became a best seller on Amazon out of over a million other designs! So, we printed up more designs. By the end of our first year in business our little hobby had brought in enough revenue to purchase a brand-new SUV outright.

Tom and I co-wrote a children's book that I illustrated, *Starfish on the Beach* that became an Amazon best seller as well. Non-profit organizations have gifted our book to volunteers to show appreciation for their work. School districts have used it to launch year-long themes of how one person can make a difference. Literacy programs have featured our book to inspire children. Like Diane Dresback, I had finally brushed off my professor's dire prediction and found success in illustration. Twice.

The Psychologist

Robert Sternberg never believed what his teachers told him about himself, even from the time he was in grade school. His skeptical perspective came to a head when he was in the sixth grade and was told he failed an intelligence test.

He knew that could not be correct; tests just made him nervous and he insisted on a retake. This time he was placed in a classroom with students who were a year younger than he was and his test jitters dissipated. He did well on the test the second time he took it.

This discrepancy in his test results fascinated him and in the seventh grade he developed his own intelligence test that he named the STOMA, which stood for the Sternberg Test of Mental Ability. That would be the beginning of his trek into the study of the mind. He knew he wanted to become a psychologist.

Robert was smart and landed a National Merit Scholarship for college. He was accepted into Yale University. His parents were thrilled as they had not even completed high school. He relied on his scholarship money and financial aid to make it happen. This was an opportunity that he would not squander.

He declared his major and with great excitement dove into the studies for his first psychology course. It was everything that he hoped it would be until finals week. As he tells it, "I had planned to be a psychology major, but I bombed introductory psychology."

His professor told him he needed to choose a different major. It felt reminiscent of his situation in the sixth grade and he thought back on the mental ability test he had created as a kid. He reminded himself of his scholarships that he had earned by his scholastic aptitude and he refused to let his dream go.

Robert stayed the course and graduated with a bachelor's degree in psychology from Yale and a PhD from Stanford. Among other accomplishments he developed the Triarchic Theory of Intelligence that is studied by psychology students today.

This theory identifies three types of mental ability, only one of which, the analytical intelligence, is measured by the IQ test. The other two are practical intelligence, that enables a person to quickly know what to do in a specific setting, and creative intelligence, which gives a person a high level of adaptability in new and unusual circumstances.

He explained his own poor grades in that first year of college this way, "I'm more of a creative learner... I do very well in projects, but I was not good at memorizing all of that material in the introductory courses."

Robert Sternberg is ranked as one of the top 100 psychologists of the twentieth century. He is a past president of the American Psychological Association and has held the positions of University President, provost and professor at various colleges. He has been awarded 13 honorary doctorates from universities around the world.

He challenged not only the prevailing thoughts of his day on the measurement of intelligence, but also rejected the assessment of his teachers on his own intelligence. In doing so he opened the world of psychology to a new vision so that others are not held back.

Diane Dresback, Michael Crichton, Robert Sternberg and I discovered that it is sometimes best not to believe what is told to you, even when it is coming from an authority figure. All professors have their own sets of biases and opinions that color what they say and what they present to their classes. Their ideas are formed by their own personal worldview and experiences.

As a student you must learn and practice discernment, throwing aside what you are told that does not align with what you believe to be true. College is a place to learn *how* to think, not *what* to think. Don't let a professor's opinions thwart your dreams and goals. Opinions are not facts.

Cultivate relationships with others who will support your vision for your future. The only one who can stop you from fulfilling your dreams is you.

19

Internal Combustion: Accelerate Your Future with Internships

"Be so good they can't ignore you."
— Steve Martin

Steven always picked up the mail. It was just a habit, but lately the task held more interest for him. He was watching for a letter, the letter that said he was accepted to his number one choice for college, the University of Southern California. They had a film school that he believed was his one path to the career he wanted.

Steven flipped through the handful of envelopes and ads until his eyes fixated on the USC logo. The sunrise epitomized his future and now he had the first door in his hands. He just had to open it.

He bolted up the stairs of his house and threw all the mail on the table except this one important letter. He stuck his finger under the corner of the flap and carefully pulled it open.

He couldn't believe he was holding this letter in his hands. "Dear Applicant," it began. "We regret to inform you…" and he stared at it. His eyes clouded and the logo on the letterhead appeared to be a sun setting, not rising as he first thought, and he felt a rock form in the pit of his stomach. He was rejected.

He knew his high school grades were not stellar. In fact, he had a C average. That is probably the reason he was denied admission, he surmised. He mentally berated himself for not putting more effort into his classes. There were just so many classes that did not interest him and that he felt he would never use. Steven lapsed into a funk that took all the joy and motivation out of him.

Steven dreaded calling his "ma" who lived in Saratoga, California to tell her the bad news. After all, he had chosen to live with his father in Los Angeles just so that he could be close to USC, the college that rejected him.

His mom, Leah Adler, listened to his disappointing announcement and then matter-of-factly told him that it was the school's loss, not his. He should shred that letter and look for a school that deserved him!

She reminded Steven of his accomplishments. He had attained the rank of Eagle Scout, which was no small feat. He had earned the 21 badges, demonstrated his leadership abilities and had stayed active in the scouts for several years. Only four percent of young men in the boy scouts ever earn the leadership rank of Eagle. He was meant to do big things, she told him, even if the college didn't see it.

As she continued with her pep talk, he couldn't help but smile. He loved the way she believed in him. He was reminded of the many scout projects she encouraged him to pursue even if they caused chaos in the house. When he signed on to complete the moviemaking scout badge it was his mom who cooked a pot full of cherries until they exploded just to get the right texture for a special effect he wanted.

Steven set up the film camera that his dad bought for him and puddled the bloody cherry substance in such a way that it oozed out of the kitchen cabinets. Then he yelled, "Action," and started filming. The movie turned out well, but Steven's mom continued to discover sticky residue on those cabinets for years afterwards.

Steven's dad sat down with him and helped him make a new plan for college. He urged him to apply to California State University at Long Beach and Steven was accepted.

Although it had not been his first choice, once he was enrolled as a degree-seeking student Steven discovered that he was eligible to apply for internships. There was one at Universal Studios that particularly interested him and he pursued it. He landed an unpaid position in the film editing department.

The job itself was not what he wanted, but the environment was electric. It was painstakingly explained to him that he was not allowed access to the studios, only the editing department. Steven nodded his understanding but devised ways to get on the set.

He snuck into different areas of Universal Studios, acting like he belonged there so no one questioned him. His college ID got him onto the studio grounds, his curiosity motivated him and his craving to learn all he could about the moviemaking industry kept him energized and taking chances. He wanted to become a film director.

Being in the right place at the right time, he was offered the opportunity to make a short film and if it turned out well enough it would be shown in theaters. He wrote and directed a 26-minute film that he titled *Amblin'*. It was a boy meets girl theme that personified the hippy movement that was prevalent at that time. The film was screened at the Atlanta Film Festival displaying his talent and, more importantly, impressing the studio vice president Sidney Sheinberg.

Steven Spielberg was only 20 years old and was one semester short of earning his college degree when he was offered a contract to direct for Universal Studios. He put his college completion on hold to start his career.

Three decades later he returned to complete his BA in Film and Electronic Arts to honor and recognize the value of what he received from his time in college. He said after flipping the tassel on his mortarboard cap from right to left, "I wanted to accomplish this for many years as a thank you to my parents for giving me the opportunity for an education and a career, and as a personal note for my own family - and young people everywhere - about the importance of achieving their college education goals."

Steven Spielberg has directed many blockbusters and won numerous Oscar and Emmy awards. Some of his most recognizable and memorable films are *Jaws, Jurassic Park, Schindler's List, The Color Purple, E.T., Close Encounters of the Third Kind, Raiders of the Lost Ark* and the *Indiana Jones* series.

Steven Spielberg has been called the greatest director that ever lived and it started with an internship that was opened up to him because he was a college student.

Spielberg is not the only highly successful person to benefit from taking on an internship. Many people in a variety of careers got their start this way.

CEOs

In 2018 Mary Barra was named one of the five most powerful women in the world. However, she began her career as a factory floor intern at General Motors. She was 18 years old, working toward a BS degree in electrical engineering at Kettering University (originally called General Motors Institute). Her responsibilities were far from glamorous, but it gave her a deep understanding of the automobile industry.

She completed her bachelor's degree and went on to complete her Masters in Business Administration from Stanford Grad School of Business. She worked hard and earned her way to the top becoming the first woman CEO in the automotive business and, not so ironically, at General Motors where she first started.

Most internships require that the intern be enrolled at a college pursuing either an undergrad or graduate degree. However, Dennis Muilenburg had already completed his master's degree in aeronautics and astronautics when he was awarded an engineering internship at Boeing. This gave the company the chance to observe his work ethic and he was able to integrate with the culture there. Apparently, it was a good fit because he started his career there and eventually became Boeing's CEO.

Another CEO, Ursula Burns, made history by becoming the first African-American woman to head a Fortune 500 company (2010 – 2017). She was a master's student working on her mechanical engineering degree when she applied for and accepted an internship at Xerox Corporation.

When she graduated the company already knew how professional she was and the kind of expertise she brought to the job. She was able to walk into a full-time position. Both Burns and the company benefitted from the arrangement as proven by the fact that she eventually became the CEO of Xerox.

TV Host

Internships don't just work for engineers and film directors. Oprah Winfrey started her career with an internship at the CBS affiliate WLAC-TV in Nashville, Tennessee. She had to do some of the menial things that most interns are asked to do, from getting coffee to editing copy, but she always chose to do more than what was required of her.

She brought her enthusiastic demeanor to the job and watched and learned from the TV show hosts. When her internship ended, she was offered a full-time job where she would have face time on TV. Oprah became the first African-American female news anchor.

Fashion Designer

Fashion designer Betsey Johnson always had a whimsical way about her. She was exuberant and fun-loving and transferred that feeling into her famous designs that have continued in popularity for several decades.

She studied for one year at the Pratt Institute after high school, but felt that she did not fit in well there. The art was too serious. She transferred to Syracuse University to complete her degree and graduated with honors.

Her meteoric rise in the fashion industry began during her first summer out of college when she won an internship in the art department at *Mademoiselle* magazine, a popular publication that ran from 1935 to 2001. The editor said, "Betsey was a blond bombshell, so full of beans and so talented." With that one internship she had already gotten their attention.

One day she wrote a thank you note to the editor and drew a fanciful shoe on the card. She knew the editor loved shoes because she had seen them decorating her office. The editor took one look at that little drawing and brought it to the art director exclaiming, "Betsey can draw!"

From that day forward she was given freelance drawing assignments that were published in the magazine. This filled her portfolio with commercial work and within one year she was hired on as a designer at Paraphernalia, an unconventional fashion boutique in New York City.

Journalist

For award-winning journalist Anderson Cooper, his internship did not lead to his career, but it was still extremely valuable. During two of his summer breaks from Yale he interned with the CIA. He got to go into the offices and see the inner workings of the covert agency that most people only wonder about. However, Cooper was disappointed with his experience there. As he explained, "It was less James Bond than I hoped it would be."

His summers with the CIA did not lead to contacts and opened doors, but it did open his eyes. He realized that if he chose to pursue journalism he could go anywhere in the world and report what he saw rather than shuffling papers in secrecy in an office.

Because he hadn't interned in a news studio, he had to find a way to get his own quality stories. He created a fake press pass and traveled to the war front of various military conflicts. He got his stories published and he got noticed, but he put himself in situations where he almost lost his life as well. An internship would have been a safer way to break into the field of journalism, but his tenacity and creativity led him into the career of his choice.

BONUS: Free Report
50 Companies That Offer Internships

Download this free report with links to 50+ companies that offer internships to college students.

To download your FREE report, go to:

www. AmericasCollegeAdvisors.com/50Internships

20

Mentors Worth a Million

"One of the greatest values of mentors is the ability to
see ahead what others cannot see and to help them
navigate a course to their destination."
— John C. Maxwell

Nazik Kambar is a traveling nurse. Her specialty is in bone
marrow transplants in pediatrics. Her days are spent
comforting children and parents as they go through some
of the most emotionally wrenching days of their lives. This
is ironic because Nazik grew up without anyone to comfort
her when she needed it.

She was eight years old when she was brought to the
United States as a refugee by her parents. Every refugee
family is unique and each of their stories is different, but
the depth of loss they experience is similarly tragic.

Nazik was born in Bagdad, Iraq and lived in Jordan for a
time. She was accustomed to the dusty, hot climate of the

Middle East. When she was transplanted to Arizona the climate was the only thing that Nazik found familiar.

Her family had brought only a few pieces of clothing from her home country. She had to learn a new language, make new friends and figure out how to manage in the American school system. She had no grandparents, aunts or uncles to turn to. She had lost everything that was dear to her and her parents were too busy struggling to find their own way to provide the words of love or comfort that she desperately needed.

Nazik poured herself into learning English and worked hard through grade school and high school. Her achievements came to the attention of a teacher who introduced her to an organization called College Success Arizona (CSA). This is a program that provides scholarships and mentors to help high potential students from low income families in the state.

Her parents were absent from her life from the time she was 14 years old so she had to figure everything out on her own. She talked often with her teacher at the high school who helped her fill out the necessary forms and urged her to follow through on interviews.

When the day came that Nazik learned she had been awarded a scholarship she wept with joy! It was an indication that someone believed in her. She did not believe she would ever be able to go to college and now the impossible was coming true. She eagerly, but with some fear of the unknown, enrolled at Arizona State University.

To see college through Nazik's eyes is refreshing and inspiring. When asked what she thought was the best part of college she replied with exuberance, "Just being in college! I felt so much self-worth there."

She eagerly anticipated learning every day and expanding her mind and her life through knowledge, but it wasn't easy for her. She was taking classes full time at ASU and working two jobs to support herself. She had to deal with a lot of trials and tribulations by herself without having family to turn to. She said it was a lonely time for her.

Nazik revealed that having a mentor was a life saver. She had a monthly phone meeting with Judy, who was provided by CSA, who asked her about her courses, her grades and her assignments. They discussed her schedule and future classes. The main thing Nazik's mentor provided was motivation, support and comfort. "She was someone who always expected me to succeed."

Nazik determined early on that she wanted to be a nurse. After she got her Bachelor's degree, she enrolled at Grand Canyon University to complete her RN. It was a demanding program that pushed her to her limits. She went through discouragement, self-doubt and exhaustion. She had times when she felt she would be better off just walking away from the struggles, but she never quit and she is very grateful that she didn't.

As a nurse she looks forward to her job every day. She knows she is making a difference in the lives of children and their parents who are having to deal with a diagnosis of leukemia. She said, "I love my job! I do not think of what I am doing as a career, but as a purpose." Because her family was absent from her life, she knows the value of a kind word and has the privilege to provide those valuable words of encouragement to her patients every day.

As advisors, Tom and I have had the joy of mentoring and inspiring students for many years. We have seen our students excel as financial planners, graphic designers, event planners, authors, entrepreneurs, medical personnel and business people. Words are powerful and we get to see lives changed through our online *College Superhero Secrets* success program that we developed as a way to mentor students through college and life. However, mentors can be found in many places.

Career Services

Aubrey Blankenship was also a student at Grand Canyon University and we urged her to spend some time connecting with the counselor in Career Services. This is a campus service that is vastly underutilized but contains a wealth of resources. She was a communications major with a strong talent for writing. It felt awkward for her to make that first appointment, but the counselor asked her questions to help guide her thinking.

Once she understood Aubrey's academic strengths and desires, the career counselor directed her to an internship opportunity for a Christian newspaper. The editor gave her topics to research and assignments to write articles for them. She had to meet deadlines even when her school work was piling up or she had to study for finals.

Aubrey approached this opportunity with professionalism and worked long hours making sure she met all the deadlines. There was no paycheck, but she was rewarded with a byline (stating her name as the author) under the title of each article. The experience was worth gold on her resume. One of her articles even became the lead story on the front page!

Aubrey's published pieces rapidly filled her portfolio with professional examples of her work. As a result of that internship and the counseling of her mentor at the career center, an international magazine extended her a lucrative offer of employment before she ever graduated! While her friends were fretting over getting any job at all, Aubrey was able to walk into her career position right after graduation.

A parent, pastor, professor, professional, coach or even a grad student that inspires you can become a great mentor. If you aspire to be a nurse like Nazik, for example, find a professional nurse or a grad student in the field of nursing and ask to take them to lunch. Have questions in mind that you can ask this person about the career or the path to get there.

From Bottom to Top

Everyone was surprised when Eric C. Broyles announced that he had enrolled in college. He finished high school at the bottom of his class and not many people thought he would be able to complete his degree. However, there were people at his church that recognized his potential. They saw his heart of compassion for others and his desire to make a difference in the world. His church presented him with a scholarship. It wasn't a lot of money, but it gave him confidence just knowing that someone believed in him.

He applied for another scholarship and was awarded a more significant amount from the Kroger Co. and he felt like he could conquer the world! Eric still had to work a lot of hours to earn the additional money he needed for his tuition and living costs but he knew how to do that. He got a job selling garage doors and even installing them through the summer months.

What he didn't know was how to do well in his classes. To bridge his learning gap Eric sought out mentors and teachers on campus who taught him the study skills he needed. They were his accountability partners making sure he was doing what he needed to do in order to pass his classes.

He drank in their guidance on how to study, take notes and how to stay organized so he didn't miss an assignment. This knowledge and assistance set him up to graduate at the very top of his class at the University of Cincinnati. He even gave the valedictorian address.

Eric continued his education, eventually becoming a corporate attorney, and in 2019 Eric proved what the people at his church always knew, that he would make a difference for others. He donated one million dollars to the Eric C. Broyles Student Success Scholarship Fund at his alma mater to help other students who are pursuing their bachelor's degrees.

"I was given mentorship, training, coaching and support by a number of people," Broyles said. "I think it would be selfish of me not to continue in the very tradition that propelled me to my current status in life."

Eric's calendar still has mentoring appointments marked on it, but now, he is the mentor to rising college students.

Elon Musk

This book would not be complete without mentioning Elon Musk. He is the money and genius behind Tesla cars, SpaceX and the creator of X.Com (the precursor of PayPal). He has been described as a serial entrepreneur and is a multi-billionaire. He has had business successes and business failures, but he has survived and grown through them all.

He has a unique demeanor and actor Robert Downey Jr. met with Elon to utilize his personality as the real character model for his role as Iron Man in the 2008 film. He has been ranked in *Forbes* as one of the world's most powerful people. He is an extraordinary man with extraordinary ideas who leads world leaders, but when he was in college, he sought out mentors too.

Elon moved from his birthplace of South Africa to Canada when he was 19 with no plans for his future. He spent one year working in difficult labor jobs. One required him to shovel out steaming hot sand and goop from a lumber mill boiler room while wearing a hazmat suit. Finally, he enrolled in Queen's University in Kingston, Ontario. By then his brother Kimbal had joined him.

In trying to find their way the two brothers would read the newspaper looking for leaders in the community that they would like to meet. Once identified, they called that person's office asking for a lunch appointment to interview him or her. They called the head of marketing for the Toronto Blue Jays baseball team. They called editors and writers for the *Globe and Mail* and executives of various businesses. They got a lot of no's, but a few yeses as well.

When the brothers landed a lunch appointment, they prepared beforehand by writing down well thought out questions and arrived on time. One successful appointment came as a result of six months of persistent calling and repeated requests. They were finally granted a meeting with Peter Nicholson, a top executive at the Bank of Nova Scotia.

Their professionalism and politeness impressed Nicholson. He said of the meeting, "I became more impressed and fascinated as I talked to them. They were so determined." In this unorthodox way, Elon had landed his first mentor. Nicholson offered him a summer internship at the bank and Elon turned to Nicholson as his financial advisor for many years.

Warren Buffett

If you are not bold enough to cold call people you read about in the news you can look closer to home. Parents can be good mentors as well.

Warren Buffett, who is far wealthier than Elon Musk, tells in his biography that his dad was his first and best mentor. His dad encouraged him to love books and investing. His father was in the investment business so there was a plethora of books on the subject at his office that Warren was welcome to borrow. He read many of them.

His dad also instilled in him a dedication to character and integrity. "The best advice I've ever been given is by my father," he said, "who told me it took 20 years to build a reputation and 20 minutes to lose it. If you remember that you'll do things differently." But he and his dad did not always see eye to eye on what the right path was for Warren's life.

Even as a child Warren was interested in business and making money. When he was in grade school and browsing through the books in the Omaha Public Library, he found the book *One Thousand Ways to Make $1000.*

That book inspired many of his early money-making ventures. He sold chewing gum to his friends and weekly magazines to his neighbors. As a teenager he delivered newspapers and made money detailing cars.

In high school he and a friend bought a used pinball machine for $25 and placed it in the local barber shop. With the money the machine generated they purchased several more machines and placed them in other barber shops. Within the year his business was showing a profit so the two turned around and sold it to a war veteran to manage. This gave Warren money to invest in other ventures. His bank account was growing.

When Warren graduated high school, he planned to dive right into his business ventures, but his dad did not approve. He insisted that Warren get his college degree first. Begrudgingly he complied. Warren pushed through his courses and by age 19 he had graduated with a Bachelor of Science in Business Administration.

Warren had a growing interest in the stock market and found another book that inspired him. It was *The Intelligent Investor* by Benjamin Graham. He became captivated by it. He read and re-read the book several times. He chose to go back to school to get his Master of Science in Economics from the Columbia Business School because he wanted the author, who was a professor there, to teach and mentor him.

"Ben Graham was certainly the man who set me on the course that's worked now for a good many years," Warren said, "Ben was this incredible teacher. It was like learning baseball from a fellow who was batting .400. It shaped my professional life."

Warren Buffett worked as an investment salesman after getting his master's degree and later became a securities analyst. He invested money that he earned and learned more about the industry. He even approached his former professor asking if he could work for him for free. Graham refused, but later hired him to work in his company for an impressive salary. Warren stayed there and absorbed all that he could learn from this brilliant man.

In 2018 Warren Buffett was ranked as the third richest man in the world behind Jeff Bezos, CEO of Amazon and Bill Gates, co-founder of Microsoft. He is considered to be one of the most successful investors ever with a net worth of

$87.5 billion. He attributes much of his success to the mentoring of both his dad and his professor.

Many students have told Tom and me that they believe asking for help is a sign of weakness. In reality, it is a sign of wisdom. If someone knows how to open a door that you want to go through, why would you try to crowbar it open? Save yourself the time and frustration by asking for the key from a mentor.

21

When All Else Fails, Work Hard

"When you start to realize that the easy way out isn't getting
you anywhere it's a terrifying yet oddly satisfying feeling."
— Ryan T. Schneider

After relinquishing all her personal items, Deborah walked
down the cold concrete hallway wearing an orange striped
jump suit. She heard the clang of the iron-barred door
shut and lock behind her. How did this young woman who
graduated college with a 4.0 GPA end up in jail?

Hard work!

Deborah grew up in Georgia and thought she would one
day like to stand in a courtroom fighting for defendants
who were unjustly accused of a crime. She cared about
people and she loved hearing their stories.

When she was a senior in high school, she entered the Junior Miss beauty contest for her town. It gave her the opportunity to present herself in a professional manner and speak before an audience and judges. She knew it would build her confidence; she didn't know she would win. She was chosen for the title of Georgia Junior Miss and propelled into the Junior Miss America competition representing her state. She said it was a huge learning experience.

The part that fascinated her the most was the way the competition was run. She watched the CBS cameramen glide the cameras into position for various shots. Huge spotlights were adjusted, and the microphones were tested for clarity of sound and then retested. She listened intently as the directors ordered people about to adhere to the strict time frames that the Junior Miss America show required. It was exciting, intense and demanding.

Although she did not win the national competition, she knew that she wanted to live in this world. She left law behind to study television journalism.

Motivated by this new direction for her life she dedicated herself to her studies, completing her degree in three years with straight A's in all of her courses. However, because of her interest in people and their stories and her interest in law, she also served on the Main Court of the University of Georgia's Student Judiciary.

Eager to get a start in the TV industry, she sought out opportunities and landed a part-time position as an intern reporter with Georgia Public Television. Ironically, even though she was no longer pursuing a degree in law, her job was to interview the state lawmakers for a show that covered all the proceedings of the Georgia General Assembly.

She did her job so well that she was noticed by an executive of WAGA-TV in Atlanta. He asked if she would be interested in a summer internship with their station. She was delighted and signed the paperwork committing herself to three months at the station.

Her first big break came less than one week into her summer job when the TV studio found themselves short on reporters. They said, "Deborah can do this," and put her in front of a camera. She shook off her nervousness and delivered the 6 o'clock evening news. Deborah had proven herself again.

Because of her great performance on the evening news she was offered the job of weekend reporter. Her dreams were moving forward faster than she ever imagined they could, and she said "yes" before she thoroughly thought through what the scheduling repercussions would be once her classes started up in the fall. She still had one year of courses to complete before she graduated from the university.

The university was in Athens, GA. The weekend job was in Atlanta, 60 miles away, but Deborah never saw this opportunity as an either/or situation. She believed she could be both a weekend reporter and a full-time college student.

As she tells it, she would complete her final class on Friday and rush to her car to drive to Atlanta. She couldn't afford a hotel room, so she would sometimes stay with a friend. The weekends when that plan didn't work out, she parked her car in the studio parking lot and slept there.

She worked every Saturday and Sunday until the completion of the 11 pm news show. Then she would drive back to Athens to be in her seat for the Monday morning class. She said it was exhausting, but she proved to herself that she could do more than she ever imagined.

During this time, she reported on the notorious Atlanta child killer who had terrorized the area for two years. She also interviewed President Jimmy Carter live on air. When she graduated, she was awarded a position as a full-time reporter. All her hard work was paying off!

And then she went to jail.

By 2000 Deborah Norville had won two Emmy awards. She had been a news anchor and an investigative reporter working for NBC, ABC, and CBS. She had authored a self-help book for women and was a household name on *Inside Edition*. That is when her editor sentenced her to one week behind bars in the toughest jail in America - not as a reporter, but as an inmate. He wanted her to experience what the incarcerated women see, feel, and hear. Deborah agreed to do it.

She did not receive any special treatment and there were moments that were scary and days that were disheartening. She was required to do the labor jobs that were demanded of all the inmates. She ate what the inmates ate and longed to see the outdoors. That one week seemed far longer than seven days.

Years earlier, when she first started college, she was driven by the desire to listen to the life stories of others. In prison she was able to hear from her fellow inmates; women who saw this as just an expected part of life. She said, "It was physically harder than I thought, but emotionally much more fulfilling than I expected." When she was released, she advocated for ways in which inmates could be given vocational courses and classes in decision-making to stop the cycle of returning to jail.

Inside Edition continues to be one of the most watched shows on television, and in 2020 Deborah Norville will celebrate 25 years as host of the show.

"FlyGirl"

Vernice Armour wiped the sweat from her brow to keep it from rolling into her eyes and blurring her vision. It was 123 degrees in the Cobra helicopter that was flying a search mission above the Iraqi desert. A squad of Marines and soldiers were depending on her to be their protector in the sky, but she could not see them.

Vernice and her team were keenly aware that they were in a high-risk area. One of their helicopters had been shot down a few days earlier. Regardless of the danger, they were maintaining an altitude of only five hundred feet while searching for the men who were being pummeled by mortar fire. They knew that the troops were out of ammunition and did not even have smoke to mark their position.

Suddenly she saw a tiny flash of light. "I've got 'em," she announced. The Marines were using a small mirror to signal their location to the helicopter.

The pilot circled back around and found the enemy's stronghold, a building with a blue dome on top. She saw the flash of enemy fire emitting from the tower and sighted the building on her target screen. Armed and ready, with adrenaline coursing through her veins she pulled the trigger.

Nothing happened.

She reported to the men in the cockpit that the weapon had failed to fire. Vernice had to settle herself. Thoughts flooded her mind of the brave troops on the ground that were counting on her to save their lives. She must not fail. She took a deep breath, reset the weapons system and squeezed the trigger a second time.

There was a flash from the explosion and flying debris, followed by a cloud of smoke that filled her nostrils with an acrid scent. "Way to go, 'FlyGirl!'" shouted the pilot. Vernice knew she had hit her mark and her mission was accomplished. The Marines and soldiers would be able to continue on.

After Vernice returned to her home base in California she was required to complete a physical at the base hospital. As she stood in line to speak to the receptionist, she began a conversation with a Marine who was standing in front of her. He told her he was there for physical therapy. He was recovering from a shrapnel injury he received while on a mission in Iraq. As the conversation continued, she realized that he was one of those soldiers rescued because of her 2003 mission in Iraq!

"I'm the pilot who pulled the trigger," she said. The young Marine looked intently at her as though he was memorizing her face.

"Ma'am," he replied, "you saved my life."

Vernice had never intended to join the military. She had always planned to be a police officer and when she was a freshman in college all she really wanted to do was party. She discovered a poster in the student union building announcing a free trip to the Mardi Gras and she was interested. When she read the details of the offer, she learned that she would first be required to join the Women's ROTC Rifle Team to qualify for the trip.

Partying at Mardi Gras was what attracted her, but learning to shoot a rifle and training with the ROTC seemed to align with her goal of becoming a police officer. She signed the contract.

Her involvement on the rifle team inspired her to sign up for the Army Reserves and Vernice pushed herself to be the best in every endeavor. Every day she awoke long before anyone else in her residence hall even stirred. She ran miles, lifted hundreds of weights and practiced her skills with guns. Her motto was "Do what average people do, you'll have what average people have," and Vernice Armour was determined to never be average. It was the fuel that kept her going.

She made sure her childhood dream to become a police officer became a reality too. While she was still completing her college degree, she put in the extra time and training to earn her badge as the first African-American female member of Nashville's motorcycle squad.

After she graduated, she moved to Arizona and served as the first African-American female police officer in Tempe. Still, she felt the need to do something bigger.

She became an officer candidate for the Marine Corps. It was on the 2003 mission to Iraq that she saved several lives. She was recognized as America's first African-American female combat pilot.

Her list of accomplishments is impressive and it all came from hard work and dedication.

- She became the first African-American female to become a member of the Nashville Police Officer's motorcycle squad – while she was still completing her college degree
- After graduation she became the first African-American female to serve as a police officer in Tempe AZ

- At Camp Pendleton while training to fly the AH-1W Super Cobra she was named Female Athlete of the Year
- Twice won Camp's Strongest Warrior Competition
- In 2003 she flew in the invasion of Iraq becoming America's first African-American female combat pilot

SwineTech

Farm work is some of the hardest work one can ever do, especially when working with animals. The job of caring for livestock is a 24/7 responsibility whether the farmer feels like doing it or not. In freezing rain, snow, or sweltering heat the animals' very survival depends upon the farmer's diligence to feed, water, and even assist with births.

This is the life that Matthew Rooda was born into. He had his own demanding chores and he watched his father and grandfather's daily hard work. He learned that the life of a farmer also required innovation and creativity to solve the many issues that arose on a farm.

As a young adult he enrolled at Hawkeye Community College and was given the opportunity to serve as an assistant farm manager in Waterloo, Iowa. He discovered that a huge problem in the field of raising pigs was that the sows had a habit of rolling over on their piglets and crushing them to death. He began to search for a way to prevent this calamity.

When he graduated with his Associates of Liberal Arts Degree, he transferred to the University of Iowa to study genetic and biotechnology. He could not forget the tragic sight he witnessed of dozens of piglets crushed by their mothers. There had to be a solution.

He teamed up with his best friend Abraham Espinoza, a computer science and engineering student from Mexico to see if they could find a way to prevent such losses in the pork industry. They conducted interviews and did their own research gathering statistics about this problem in the industry. They determined that 92% of pork producers were looking for a solution to the problem of piglets being crushed.

Rooda and Espinoza presented their idea to the Iowa Startup Accelerator and were one of only nine start-up companies out of hundreds of applicants to be welcomed into the program. This program gave them help with research, development of their ideas and even business expertise.

This was an intense 90-day program that necessitated their dropping out of college for one semester. They used the time to develop the technology that would solve this problem. They brought another partner on board and were able to create an algorithm that could recognize the particular sound a piglet makes when it is being squashed.

They next needed to develop a way to cause the sow to stand up, thereby freeing the piglet. Their goal was to create a prod to alert the sow that would be no more stressful to the momma pig than a pair of hands nudging her.

Through trial and error, they had a prototype ready to test by the time the three-month Start-up Accelerator program ended. The two students re-enrolled in the university and continued their education by attending night classes while working diligently with the pigs during the day. The long days Matthew spent working on his studies and his fledgling business were reminiscent of the hours he saw his father work on the farm. He was not about to give up.

Abraham named their company SwineTech and farmers who used their SmartGuard product reported a nearly 60% reduction in piglets being crushed. Before graduating Rooda and Espinoza's company was recognized as one of Forbes 30 under 30 most promising companies in Manufacturing and Industry. They even received awards from MIT, the National Inventors Hall of Fame and the American Farm Bureau Federation.

Within the first year of existence SwineTech was able to protect tens of thousands of litters of piglets. Their hard work changed the industry and launched their careers.

Deborah Norville, Vernice Armour and the co-founders of SwineTech recognized the need to work longer hours than any of their peers to reach the goals they wanted. Oftentimes just doing a little bit more than the "next guy" is enough to push you to the top of the achievers.

Sometimes, however, you have to do a lot more.

22

Keys to Launching a Great Life

"Every great dream begins with a dreamer. Always remember, you have within you the strength, the patience, and the passion to reach for the stars to change the world."
— Harriet Tubman

When embarking on a college career one tends to think that the goal is to scale Mount University and plant one's flag on the pinnacle of success. That flag is the degree, that statement that says you did it! Bands play, graduation caps are thrown into the air and the world comes knocking at your door to glean from your new-found wisdom.

Full disclosure, it does not happen that way. Instead of getting an admission ticket to zipline onto the moving train of your career, all too often the degree is a stopping point. It is the end of many years of hard work and the point where graduates scratch their heads and say, "Now, what do I do?"

When students enroll in college, they are given an advisor whose job it is to help them choose a major and to complete the requirements that will give them a degree in that major. The advisor's job is not to make sure the student gets a career. The advisor provides the student with a "to do" list to get them from enrollment to graduation. It is simply a checklist of what they need to do to get their degree.

As a newly enrolled student he or she is told the courses they must take to attain the degree. The start of each course includes a syllabus that lists the papers that the student must write and tests that must be passed. The student is told the number of points that must be earned for each project to pass the course. It is all laid out clearly. The list of requirements changes only if the student changes majors.

The student is left with the impression that all they have to do is complete the instructions, follow the rules and they are guaranteed a career job upon graduation. Just get the degree and they are on the road to success.

But what if I told you that the degree is not the goal? College is just one piece of the journey toward launching a successful career and life.

This book is filled with over 90 stories of people who have become highly successful, each in the field of their choosing. College played a part in each of their successes. Some got degrees and some did not. Some knew what they wanted to achieve before they ever started their college career. Others stumbled upon their destiny with the help of people they met in the highly creative environment of college life. But each of them would most likely never have achieved their level of success if they had never attended college.

The successful people profiled in this book came from a wide range of backgrounds. Some like Liz Murray came from very poor families. Others like Brian Scudamore came from a home that could afford to send him anywhere he wanted to go. Many like Denzel Washington and Ashton Kutcher came from households where their parents divorced, leaving them with emotional and financial fallout. Others came from supportive homes with two parents to love and encourage them. You may have noticed that some attended Ivy League schools and others went to community colleges or state schools.

Steven Spielberg, like many students, did not get accepted into the college he had set his hopes on. He instead went to a different college and still found the doors to open that launched his career.

There is one common thread that runs through all of these success stories, however. The students became convinced that their lives had a purpose. They believed they were meant to do something that would make life better for others. Then they set about to find that purpose and pursued it with intentionality. No matter who you are or where you are coming from, these secrets to success can work for you too.

What's in It for You?

So, what can you take from this book to help you launch your own success?

Whether you are a student soon to enter college or someone who never intends to enroll, there are lessons to be learned from those who have walked before you. Tom and I have seen single moms who wanted to improve their lives, businessmen who wanted to boost their careers, students in college and students in high school find success by using these exact tips. They are life and leadership tools to help you rise above the crowd.

Take the examples of the lives of successful people that you read about in the pages of this book and intentionally follow in their footsteps. Just like setting out a path of peanuts will lead squirrels right to your door, intentionally using just one or two of the secrets found in this book will lead success to your life. To help you do that here is a summary of the secrets found in this book that can lead you to a great life.

1. Create a Plan

Whatever you would like to achieve or wherever you would like to go, you need to first start with a plan. Brian Scudamore believes that the very act of writing down your goals and plans will generate thoughts and observations that can help you achieve those goals. You need to be flexible, however. Just as Julie Marie Carrier discovered that she would be happier working with children than with animals, you may discover new passions and pathways as well.

Writing down a goal does not set it in stone, but it does start you moving forward. Once you are moving toward a goal you will more quickly see new opportunities or directions and modify your focus. When a boat is moving forward in the water, one small adjustment of the rudder will turn the boat easily. If the boat is sitting still, however, you can turn the rudder as much as you want but the boat will continue to point in the same direction.

Start moving forward with the best plan you have right now and adjust it as you learn new things. If at some point you decide to drop out of college, do so with a solid plan in place as to where you are going next.

You must always have a destination in mind in order to keep moving forward. Don't drop out of college with the idea that "I'll figure out what I'm going to do once I am no longer in school." Dropping out with no plan is a plan to fail.

2. Practice Professionalism

I like telling students that two words led to fame and fortune for me. I said "thank you" when it was least expected. Gratitude and graciousness are twins that you should bring with you everywhere you go. People are drawn to others who are thoughtful and thankful.

Actor Glenn Morshower took a bad situation and turned it into a blessing that would last for many years just by acting professionally with grace and a gentle demeanor.

Airline pilot Susan Amstutz tells new college students to think of their time on campus as a four-year interview. Professors and other students are making judgements about you based on your attitude and demeanor.

This is not confined to the college campus. Whether you are on the job, out shopping, or at a social gathering people are forming opinions about you based on your behavior and words. These opinions determine if they would like to spend more time with you, introduce you to their friends and associates or even offer you a job. One introduction could change the trajectory of your life for the better.

3. Create a Social Network

In *The Happiness Advantage*, author Shawn Achor makes the argument that social support is your single greatest asset. He says that evidence from decades of research shows that there is "only one characteristic that distinguished the happiest 10 percent from everybody else; the strength of their social relationships." However, it takes effort and choice to spend time getting to know other people.

As you have discovered in this book, it was through intentionally developing social relationships that many successful businessmen and women found their business partners. It was through social engagement that a brand-new novelist was able to call the president of the United States and get an endorsement for his book. Individuals have found life-long friends and job opportunities just by showing interest in other people.

Use the technique that both former presidents George W. Bush and Bill Clinton used to remember other people's names. It is one of the simplest and yet most powerful ways to build a connection with someone else.

4. Let Go of Perfectionism

Researchers have reported that people who were insistent upon attaining perfect scores throughout their school years tended to take that perfectionist mindset into the rest of their lives. The A-achiever is often seen by potential employers as someone who is rigid and may not be able to work well as a team member, focusing instead on their own personal success without regard for others.

Hart Research Associates reported that "large majorities [of employers] say they are more likely to consider a job candidate who has participated in an internship, senior project, collaborative research project, field-based project ...or community-based project."

That means that the student should spend some time doing other things than just studying to be especially attractive to future employers. However, doing so may cause a grade or two to be lower than an A+. This can be a challenge for some people, but is an essential skill to learn for future success. C's, however, are *not* better than A's!

To fully utilize the opportunities that are available in college you need to make time to get involved with extracurricular activities and that may mean allowing good enough to be good enough, as actress Sami Gayle discovered.

The one caveat is if you intend to pursue medical school or law school, then strive to get as many A's as possible, but don't focus solely on your grades. Your social and extra-curricular activities are also important factors in getting that medical or law school admission.

5. Learn to Laugh

In this book you discovered how John Krasinski's college life was enhanced by joining a comedy troupe. Michael Dubin credits his improv class as having more to do with the success of the billion-dollar company he created than any of his other college courses. These comedy opportunities taught them how to laugh at themselves and how to generate laughter and goodwill in others.

One of the best things you can do for your life is to learn to laugh. Life can be stressful whether you are trying to accomplish your goals or you have reached a level of success. The stress just keeps coming.

Find a way to laugh about your circumstances. Laugh about your own mistakes and find a way to bring joy to others. Your body rewards you when you laugh by flooding your body with feel-good endorphins. You reward others when you smile.

People are drawn to happy people, so smile, laugh often, and you will discover your life becomes more rewarding and more fulfilling. You will even find you'll have better relationships.

6. Take Advantage of What You Have Now

No matter where you are in life, whether in school or in a career, there are opportunities that you have right now that will not always be there. Too many people get stuck in the destructive pattern of complaining about what they don't have while missing what they do have.

Does your company offer a free fitness program or a financial matching program? Take advantage of it! Does your college offer access to business equipment or a green screen? Learn how to use these tools. You never know when you may need this knowledge in the future.

Wendy Williams learned everything she could at the student-run radio station. That experience prepared her for her award-winning career on TV. Cavin Gray learned every aspect of the film making business while at Scottsdale Community College, never imagining he would become the documentary filmmaker for Phoenix Children's Hospital.

Missy Franklin, Katie Ladecky, and Zach Allen knew that being a college student gave them the golden opportunity to win awards and set records for their universities while building connections with teammates that would last a lifetime. They chose that over millions of dollars in endorsements. They could earn money the rest of their lives.

Don't miss out on the present by bemoaning the past or longing for the future. Today is rich with possibilities.

Grab hold of them so that you don't have regrets tomorrow.

7. Be Willing to Compete

College is a great time to test your abilities in a variety of competitions. My co-author Tom Schneider ended up traveling around the world just from auditioning for a singing group. Carrie Underwood took the microphone for *American Idol* just to see if she could do it and she won!

Some colleges offer business competitions. Challenge yourself to come up with an innovative solution to a common problem and enter it. It may launch you into a successful business venture as it did for siblings Jake and Caroline Danehy. Whether you win or not, just by preparing for a competition will help you develop your ideas and polish your skills.

If you are not in college, many competitions come in the form of job interviews, writing submissions, marathon races or community theater auditions. Push yourself to try something new.

Many people have told me they would love to write a book someday. I tell them to start by writing an article and submitting it to a magazine. See what topics *Chicken Soup for the Soul* is requesting on their website and write a story to submit to them following their guidelines. One of my stories that was published in *Chicken Soup for the Soul* got me featured on national TV.

If you have ever wanted to act, your local theaters seek actors of all ages. Learn what they need from you to audition. Then prepare, practice and do it! You could even try your skills at singing or stand-up comedy at a local open mic night.

Never stop competing. Your biggest opponent is yourself and your fears. Break through the inertia, challenge yourself and you may discover a whole new world.

8. Don't Let Failure Stop You

While we are on the subject of competing, we need to also talk about failing. So many great things come from failure if you build upon that loss to take you to the next level. Failure is not the end; it is the beginning of something new.

Getting fired or having to face the devastating loss of a dream can be an opportunity to rethink and reinvent your life, as NFL player Trent Shelton did. HGTV would never have seen the record numbers of viewership that Chip Gaines brought if he had not been stopped from pursuing his dream of having a major league baseball career.

Life is not linear. Whether you fail to reach a goal you set for yourself or life throws detours and disasters in your way that you never expected, there will come a time when you have to stop your forward motion.

Force yourself to forge a new path like Bernie Fuchs did. He had no choice but to give up his future as a trumpet player when he lost his fingers. He chose to learn a new skill and thrilled the world though his paintings and illustrations instead. Being forced to change your focus and direction is painful and difficult, but it can lead to an even better future than you could have ever imagined.

9. Look Outside of Your Own Needs

Paul Orfalea did not dwell on the fact that he could barely read or write. Instead he chose to see his learning disability as a motivation to build teams of people to help each other. He completed college and built the Kinkos empire with a team of people he recruited. He focused on what others needed - convenient access to copiers - and set out to provide that.

Zach Winkler noticed a need on campus and invented a way to keep his fellow students safe. Inadvertently he ended up launching a multi-million-dollar business that has been instrumental in saving many lives.

Michael Skinner met an Uber driver who lamented that his daughter was born without hands and he could not afford prosthetics for her. Michael used the equipment at his college to create inexpensive custom prosthetics for the girl and better honed his own engineering skills in the process.

Emily Kennedy did not have the technology skills to solve the problem that tugged at her heart, but she forged ahead with an idea. She wanted to find a way to use AI to find and rescue the victims of sex trafficking. Like Paul, she had to find the people who had the knowledge and ability she lacked. Her program, Traffic Jam, has helped law enforcement agencies improve their efficiency in investigations by 50%, enabling them to take down many organized criminal networks and rescue victims.

There will always be problems to solve. You may be the one that finds the solution, or like Ashton Kutcher, be the one that funds the solution. Sometimes you will need other people to help you, and sometimes other people will need you. Either way, you can help to change the world for the better.

10. Volunteer

Every non-profit, church or club can use volunteers. Choose to help a program that resonates with you, whether it has anything to do with your career focus or not. One student I know likes to volunteer her time to just sit and hold the premature babies at the hospital. It solves an important need for the child and the student finds it to be an amazing stress-reliever for her.

Some volunteer opportunities require specialized skills like building a website, fund-raising, teaching, building houses, or writing copy. Whatever your expertise you can offer it and build your resume at the same time. Many volunteers have made invaluable connections that led to great career jobs. Others have just satisfied their personal need to make a difference.

11. Think for Yourself

One of the hardest parts of adulting is to develop your ability to discern truth. Many college students push their parents away to prove they can find their own way. Unfortunately, these very same students often replace their parents with someone new to follow.

You are a leader, or you would not have picked up this book. Your desire is to make a difference in the world and as Captain Picard of the Starship Enterprise used to say, "Go where no man has gone before." To do that you have to think for yourself and not allow others to tell you what to think, not even your professors.

Every person has a worldview that shapes their choices and as an adult you must determine yours. Your professor may be cynical from disappointments in his or her life and what that instructor espouses will be colored by their experiences. They may tell you that "no one can succeed in that field" like some of the people you read about in this book. Those professors were proven wrong.

Your experiences may be entirely different. Stand your ground on what you believe. When you are confronted by an opposing view, listen, but also do some research for yourself. Get input from a variety of sources with different perspectives. Do not just accept what the loudest voice is screaming.

The values and worldview you adapt will influence your decisions and choices in all aspects of your life. It is essential that you determine who you are, who you want to become, and what you want your legacy to be.

12. Find an Internship

Most internships are only offered while a student is enrolled in college. Unlike volunteering, you need to find opportunities to intern in a career field that interests you. The CEOs of many top companies began by filing papers, fetching coffee, editing film or even sweeping floors as an intern. It not only gives you a look inside the inner workings of companies that are otherwise closed to the general public, but you also get the chance to meet the movers and shakers of the industry.

Once in an internship, dress to fit in and work to stand out. Approach any internship - even an unpaid one - as an extended job interview. Work hard and do more than expected. By doing an internship well many students like Mary Barra, the CEO of General Motors, have proven themselves to be a professional that the company does not want to lose.

13. Connect with a Mentor

The most successful people in the world rely on mentors to guide them throughout their lives. Having a successful life is only possible by continuously making good choices as circumstances change around you.

Having someone who can give you sound advice is essential. Couples seek marriage counselors and pastors to establish and strengthen loving relationships. CEOs of businesses pay advisors to keep their companies on track. Managers and teachers participate in trainings.

I would urge you to find a mentor as well. These may be professional counselors or advisors or just someone you trust who has walked the path you are walking. A mentor can help you avoid the pitfalls that have confounded many others and accelerate your progress.

As America's College Advisors, parents hire us to ensure their young adults successfully navigate "the dangerous decade of decision-making" because most become lost, lonely or left behind between the ages of 18 and 28. We help them launch a plan of action for a great life, powerful relationships and lucrative careers through our online life success mentoring program called *College Superhero Secrets*. In this 8-module program we lead you through everything you will need to do *in* college to be successful *after* college and to have a solid job offer before you even graduate.

Each module focuses on a different success principle and each lesson includes an Action Plan which will help you apply what you are learning to lead you along the path to success. We have helped thousands of students through some of the most difficult decisions of their lives. We would count it a privilege to be your mentor as well through *College Superhero Secrets*.

For more information about this success mentoring program visit:

www.CollegeSuperheroSecrets.com

You can also get more information by visiting our website:

www.AmericasCollegeAdvisors.com

There are lots of additional free resources and helpful tips on this site that can prepare you for success in college, career, relationships and life.

One Final Thought – D.O.T.

Throughout this book you have seen what others have done to launch their success. Now it is up to you to launch your own. You don't have to do all thirteen things. In fact, we recommend you only choose one thing to start. That's it. Start with D.O.T., Do One Thing. When you have had success with laughing and looking at life in a more positive way, for example, then add one more thing.

You don't need to employ every secret found in this book to achieve success (though the more of them you do the more likely success will come your way). James Clear, the author of *Atomic Habits* states that, "if you can get one percent better each day for one year, you'll end up thirty-seven times better by the time you're done."

Transformation comes slowly and we often do not see the benefit of doing one small thing, but if you are consistent and intentional to continue in that one thing you will see a compounding benefit.

The secrets you've discovered in this book provide you with a playbook that can lead you to success in whatever endeavor you pursue, but it will take intentionality, purpose and a passion to succeed.

We cannot guarantee you the life of your dreams. There will always be unforeseen circumstances that can cause you to make changes, but the secrets you learn here can help you overcome them and still find the happiness, satisfaction and success in your life you desire.

Our sincere hope is that you apply the D.O.T concept every day and take the success secrets from this book to shape your future. And if you want to go deeper into many of these success principles and more, don't hesitate to reach out to us at:

support@AmericasCollegeAdvisors.com

We wish you all the best in your future, and much success.

Where They Went to College

Allen, Paul	Washington State
Allen, Zach	Boston College
Amstutz, Susan	U of Oklahoma
Armour, Vernice	Middle Tennessee State University
Atkinson, Rowan (Mr. Bean)	Newcastle, Queens College, Oxford
Ballmer, Steve	Harvard College
Bareilles, Sara	UCLA
Barra, Mary	Kettering U, Stanford Grad School of Bus.
Berkowitz, Seth	U of Pennsylvania
Bird, Brad	CA Institute of the Arts
Blair, Tal	U of St. Augustine, FL
Blankenship, Aubrey	Grand Canyon University
Booker-Drew, Froswa'	U of Texas, Arlington
Broyles, Eric C.	U of Cincinnati, U of Virginia Law School
Buffett, Warren	U of Pennsylvania, U of Nebraska, Columbia U, Institute of Finance
Burns, Ursula	Brooklyn Polytechnic Institute, Columbia
Bush, George W.	Yale, Harvard Bus. School
Caplan, Thomas	Georgetown, Harvard Bus. School
Carrier, Julie Marie	Ohio State
Chan, Priscilla	Harvard, U of C Med School
Christianson, Robert	Arizona State

Clinton, Bill	Georgetown, Oxford, Yale Law School
Cooper, Anderson	Yale
Crichton, Michael	Harvard College, Harvard Medical School
Danehy, Caroline	Colgate and LIM
Danehy, Jake	Colgate
Deming, Laura	Mass Institute of Tech
Dresback, Diane	Cal State Fullerton, U of Phoenix
Dubin, Michael	Emory
Espinoza, Abraham	U of Iowa
Fazzina, Daniel	St. Johns, NY
Franklin, Missy	UC Berkeley
Fuchs, Bernie	Washington, St. Louis MO
Full Goh, Eden	Princeton
Gaines, Chip	Baylor
Gates, Bill	Harvard College
Gayle, Sami	Columbia
Gore, Al	Harvard College
Grabowski, Cole	Notre Dame
Gray, Cavin	Scottsdale Community College, Azusa Pacific
Hudak, Taylor	U Connecticut
Izzo, Tom	Northern MI, Marquette
Jacobson, Sam	USC
Jobs, Steve	Reed College
Johnson, Betsey	Pratt Institute, Syracuse
Jones, Tommy Lee	Harvard College
Kambar, Nazik	AZ State, Grand Canyon U
Kennedy, Emily	Carnegie Mellon
Kenyon, Cynthia	University of Georgia, MIT
King, Stephen	University of Maine
Krasinski, John	Brown U
Kunnemann, Aaron	University of Missouri

Kutcher, Ashton	University of Iowa
Kutcher, Michael	Mount Mercy
Ladecky, Katie	Stanford
Lasseter, John	Pepperdine, CA Inst. of the Arts
Lawson Hardy, Renee	Texas U, Austin
Luan, David	Yale
Mackey, John	Texas U, Austin, Trinity
Malinchak, James	University of Cincinnati, University of Hawaii, Hilo
Mariucci, Steve	Northern Michigan, Marquette
Marshall, Thurgood	Lincoln, Howard U School of Law
Middleton, Kate	Marlborough College, University of St Andrews, Fife, Scotland
Momoa, Jason	Des Moines Area CC, CO State, University of HI
Muilenburg, Dennis	Iowa State, Washington U
Murbach, John	Wake Forest
Murray, Liz	Harvard College
Musk, Elon	Queens University, U of PA
Norville, Deborah	University of Georgia
Orfalea, Paul	USC
Pacifico, Kelly	Notre Dame
Ramono, Ray	Queens College, NY
Rhames, Ving	State U of NY at Purchase, Julliard School
Rooda, Matthew	Hawkeye CC, U of Iowa
Schneider, Jeremy	Grand Canyon U
Schneider, Lindy	Tulsa University
Schneider, Ryan	Grand Canyon U
Schneider, Tom L.	Wheaton College, Northern Illinois University

234 | College Secrets

Scudamore, Brian	Concordia, U of British Columbia
Segal, Erich	Harvard College
Selton, Trent	Baylor
Skinner, Michael	Notre Dame
Spielberg, Steven	Cal State Long Beach
Sprinkles, Jonathan	University of Texas, Austin
Sternberg, Robert	Yale
Strobel, Lee	University of MO, Yale Law School
Theil, Peter	Stanford, Stanford Law School
Tim Burton	CA Institute of the Arts
Tucci, Stanley	State U of NY, Purchase
Underwood, Carrie	NE State, Tahlequah, OK
Washington, Denzel	Fordham
Williams, Wendy	Northeastern, Boston
Windsor, Prince William	Eton College, University of St. Andrews in Fife, Scotland
Winfrey, Oprah	TN State
Winkler, Zach	University of MO
Zuckerberg, Mark	Harvard

References

Chapter 1- Expect Major Changes

(1) Rader D. (December 12, 1999). *"I Try to Send a Good Message"*. Parade Magazine.

(2) Kershaw T. (April 27, 2012). *The Religion and Political Views of Denzel Washington*, Hollowverse.

(3) Crowther, L. (January, 2013). *Explore History, Thurgood Marshall: 20 Facts*. Legacy.

(4) Biography.com Editors (April 2, 2014). *Thurgood Marshall Biography*. A&E Television Networks.

Chapter 2 - Your Career Starts IN College

(1) Malinchak J. (October 1, 1998). *From College to the Real World: Street Smart Strategies for Landing Your Dream Job and Creating a Successful Future.* Positive Publishing.

Chapter 3 - Billionaire Drop Outs

(1) The Wendy Williams Show, YouTube. (October 12, 2018). *College Dropout.*

(2) Bellis M. (December 31, 2018) *Biography of Bill Gates*. Thought Co.

(3) Moen J. YouTube. (Dec. 18, 2010). *History of Microsoft.*

(4) Shontell A. (May 30, 2014). *Mark Zuckerberg Used This Pickup Line On His Wife Back in College, And She Was "Appalled."* Business Insider.

(5) Tchir J. (June 12, 2016). *Brian Scudamore: 'Don't Think About the How While You're Dreaming."* The Globe and Mail Inc.

(6) Balfour B. (May 16, 2018). *Junk Tycoon Treasures His Bucket-List Hug with Oprah.* The Globe and Mail Inc.

(7) Mackey J. (February 1, 2007). *"I No Longer Want to Work for Money."* Fast Company.

(8) Arlidge J. (January 28, 2006). *Peace, Love and Profit – Meet the World's Richest Organic Grocer.* The Guardian.

(9) John Naughton (October 8, 2011). *"Steve Jobs: Stanford commencement address, June 2005"*. The Guardian.

Chapter 4 – Transform Your Life: Make Your Own Luck

(1) Newmark A. and Norville D. (2016). *Chicken Soup for the Soul: The Power of Gratitude: 101 Stories about How Being Thankful Can Change Your Life,* page 91. Chicken Soup for the Soul.

(2) Norville D., Inside Edition. (September 9, 2016). *How a Simple 'Thank You' Paid Off Big Time for a Woman Fired from Her Job.*

Chapter 5 – Friends with Benefits

(1) Democratic National Convention, Los Angeles, C-Span. (August 16, 2000). *Tommy Lee Jones Nominates Al Gore.* C-Span.

(2) Fogarty, L. (Sept. 16, 2015) *How Did Kate Middleton & Prince William Meet? They Might have Black Underwear to Thank.* Bustle.

(3) Texas Lutheran University, YouTube. (Oct. 29, 2015). Breaking Night – *Liz Murray from Homeless to Harvard.*

(4) Murray, L. (Sept. 7, 2010). *Breaking Night: A Memoir of Forgiveness, Survival, and My Journey from Homeless to Harvard.* Hachett Books.

Chapter 6 – The Power of Connectivity

(1) Caplan, T. and Clinton, B. (Jan. 10, 2012). *The Spy Who Jumped Off the Screen,* introduction. Penguin Books.

(2) Huddleston Jr., T. (June 15, 2018). *When 'Incredibles 2' director Brad Bird was 14 He Sent Disney a Short Film He Made in His Basement – and the Studio Liked It.* CNBC Make It.

(3) Abramowitz, R. (Feb. 17, 2008). *His Life Began at 40.* Los Angeles Times.

Chapter 7 – B's are Better Than A's

(1) Fuller. B. (May 16, 2018). *Sami Gayle Reveals How She Juggled College, 'Blue Bloods' and 'Candy Jar' – Her Insane Schedule.* Hollywood Life.

(2) Hageman, E. (July 1, 2018). *Interview/Sami Gayle.* Schon!

(3) Hudak, T. (Oct. 24, 2018). *Fresh Talk: An 'A' Student Gives Teachers 8 Pieces of Advice.* Hartford Courant.

(4) Mejia, Z. (April 29, 2018). *The No. 1 Thing Bill Gates Wishes He'd Done in College*. CNBC Make It.

(5) Sprinkles, J. (2019). *Jonathan Sprinkles.*University of Texas, Wayfinder.

(6) Akers, M. and Porter, G. (Oct. 8, 2018). *What is Emotional Intelligence (EQ)?* PsychCentral.

(7) Branson, R. (Aug. 31, 2015). *You Can't Fake Personality, Passion or Purpose*. Richard Branson on LinkedIn.

(8) Zoltners, A., Sinha, PK. And Lorimer, S. (Aug. 29, 2012). *In Sales, Hire for Personality, then Train for Skill.* Harvard Business Review.

Chapter 8 – Don't Take College Seriously

(1) Gilbey, R. (Dec. 11, 2004). *Rowan Atkinson: Mr. Bean Shows His Serious Side*. Independent.

(2) Morales-Rolon, J. (June 15, 2009). *10 Questions for John Krasinski*. Time Magazine.

(3) Lashinsky, A. (March 10, 2015). *How Dollar Shave Club Got Started*. Fortune.

(4) Denning, S. (May 31, 2018). Dollar Shave Club Founder: *Why Life is Defined by Choices*. Forbes.

(5) Frieswick, K. (April 2016). *The Serious Guy Behind Shave Club's Crazy Viral Videos*. INC.

(6) Umoh, R. (Sept. 27, 2017). *3 Things Dollar Shave Club's CEO Learned About Success from Studying Improv*. CNBC.

Chapter 9 – The Clock is Ticking

(1) Biography.com Editors (Feb. 5, 2019) *Stephen King Biography*. A&E Television Networks.

(2) Feilly, L. (Jan. 11, 2017) *How Stephen King's Wife Saved Carrie and Launched His Career*. MentalFloss.com.

(3) Videomessage777. YouTube. (Feb. 14, 2012). *CRAZY! Wendy Williams vs Whitney Houston Interview in 2003 Part One.*

(4) Radio Hall of Fame. (2009). *Talk Show Host Wendy Williams.*

Chapter 10 – Paid NOT to Go

(1) Russo, R. Associated Press (Aug. 11, 2018). *BC Star Allen Often Overlooked, Never Outworked.* The Eagle-Tribune.

(2) Dinan, T. (Mar. 5, 2018). *First Things First: Zach Allen Forgoes NFL Draft, Stays with Boston College Football.* NewCanaanAdvertiser.

(3) Clynes, T. (Feb. 22, 2017) *Peter Thiel Thinks You Should Skip College, and He'll Even Pay You for Your Trouble.* Newsweek.

(4) Loizos, C. (Feb. 2018). *This 23 Year Old Just Closed Her Second Fund – Which is Focused on Aging – with $22 Million.* Tech Crunch.

(5) Loizos, C. (Jan. 2018). *One of the Youngest Fund Managers in the U.S. Just Launched Her Own Accelerator, Too.* Tech Crunch.

(6) Chen, J. (Aug. 6, 2011). *Dropping Out and Dreaming On.* The Boston Globe.

(7) Del Valle, G. (Aug. 21, 2017). *When the Money Runs Out.* The Outline.

(8) Knapp, G. (Feb. 27, 2013). *Missy Franklin, Amateur Rock Star.* Sports on Earth.

(9) NCAA Regulations Handbook.

(10) Harris, B. Associated Press. (Jan. 11, 2018) *Missy Franklin Starting New Year, New Chapter in Georgia.* U.S. News & World Report.

(11) Gaines, C. (Aug. 24, 2016). *Katie Ledecky Explains Why She is Passing Up $5 Million Per Year in Endorsements.* Business Insider.

(12) Bloom, B. (Feb. 5, 2016). *Why Missy Franklin Turned Down $5 Million – and Does Not Regret Her Decision One Bit.* The Telegraph.

Chapter 11 – Star Wars: Competition is a Winning Thing

(1) Plautz, J. (Aug. 9, 2007*). 8 Surprising College Roommates.* Mental Floss.

(2) Winch, J. (Aug. 6, 2015). *Local Teen Entrepreneurs Turn Plastic Waste into Trendy Bathing Suits.* Westchester Magazine.

(3) Bleznak, E. (June 7, 2018). *These Secrets from Carrie Underwood's Childhood Only Make Us Love Her More.* Health & Fitness Cheatsheet.

Chapter 12 – Fail to Succeed

(1) Howes, L. (May 2018). *Trent Shelton -Show the World Your Greatness.* [Audio Podcast] LewisHowes.

Chapter 13 – Directionally Challenged

(1) Bareilles, S. (Oct. 6, 2015) *Sounds Like Me: My Life (So Far) in Song.* Simon & Schuster.

(2) Gaines, C. (Oct. 17, 2017). *Capital Gaines: Smart Things I Learned Doing Stupid Stuff.* Thomas Nelson.

Chapter 14 – You're Not the Problem – Find One

(1) Reilly, K. (March 19, 2018). *Record Numbers of College Students are Seeking Treatment for Depression and Anxiety – But Schools Can't Keep Up.* Time Magazine.

(2) Orfalea, P. as told to Marsh, A. (2005, 2007). *Copy This! How I Turned Dyslexia, ADHD, and 100 Square Feet into a Company Called Kinkos.* Workman Publishing.

(3) Casey, D. (Oct. 10, 2015). *Insomnia Cookies Caters to Late-Night Munchies.* CNBC.

(4) Kupper, C. (April 2018). *Deep Web, Deeper Faith.* Focus on the Family. Citizen Magazine

Chapter 15 – Divergent Thinking

(1) Reynolds Journalism Institute. YouTube. (May 4, 2016). *Zach Winkler Tech Showcase 2016.*

(2) Feldt, B. (April 9, 2018). *MetroLink Partners with SafeTrek Startup to Offer Commuters Safety App.* St. Louis Post-Dispatch.

Chapter 16 – The Force Awakens: Passion to Purpose

(1) University of Notre Dame. YouTube. (May 25, 2018). *Engineering Serendipity.*

(2) Hastings, D. Inside Edition (Sept. 28, 2018) *Indiana Girl Gets 3D-Printed Hands After Notre Dame Student Offers to Help.*

(3) www.ND.edu/features/e-nabled.

(4) Leadem, R. (Feb. 7, 2017). *6 Things You Can Learn from Actor, Entrepreneur and Investor Ashton Kutcher on His Birthday.* Entrepreneur.

(5) Ray, S. (Dec. 14, 2016). *From Iowa to Hollywood: The Life and Times of Actor Turned Entrepreneur, Ashton Kutcher.* Your Story.

Chapter 17 – Be Good for Nothing

(1) Canfield, J. and Switzer, J. (Jan. 27, 2015). *The Success Principles: How to Get from Where You Are to Where You Want to Be,* pg. 25. Harper Collins Publishers.

(2) Snyder, A. (April 6, 2018). *Opinion: Volunteering Now is Vital for Students in the Long-Run.* The State Press, Arizona State University.

(3) Grimm, R. T., Jr. and Dietz, N. (March 2018). *Good Intentions, Gap in Action: The Challenge of Translating Youth's High Interest in Doing Good into Civic Engagement.* Research Brief: Do Good Institute, University of Maryland.

(4) Paynter, B. (May 25, 2018). *College Kids Want to Save the World, Just Don't Ask Them to Volunteer.* Fast Company.

Chapter 18 – Don't Always Believe the Professor

(1) Smith, D. (Dec. 2, 2006). *King of the Techno-Thriller.* The Guardian.

(2) Cheery, K. (Oct. 27, 2018). *Biography of Psychologist Robert Sternberg.* VeryWell Mind.

(3) Sternberg, R.J. (2003). *Giftedness According to the Theory of Successful Intelligence.* In N.Colangelo & G. Davis (EDS.), *Handbook of Gifted Education* (88-99). Boston MA: Allyn and Bacon.

Chapter 19 – Internal Combustion: Accelerate Your Future with Internships

(1) Bernstein, F. A. (Dec. 1990). *The World is Going to Hear of this Boy.* The Jewish Mother's Hall of Fame.

(2) Japlot, P. (July 10, 2017). *When Steven Spielberg did an Internship in Universal Studios.* LetsIntern.

(3) Chavez, S. Times Staff Writer. (May 31, 2002). *Spielberg to Add B.A. to His Resume.* Los Angeles Times.

(4) Batchelor, M. (May 11, 2018). *The World's 5 Most Powerful Women for the Year 2018.* CEO World Magazine.

(5) The New York Times, staff writer. (Dec. 10, 2013) *Mary Barra, G. M.'s New Chief, Speaking Her Mind.* The New York Times.

(6) Muilenburg, D. A. (2019). *Executive Biography of Dennis A. Muilenburg.* Boeing.

(7) Nolen, J. (August 13, 2010). *Ursula Burns American Executive.* Encyclopedia Britannica.

(8) Schiro, A. (May 18, 1999) *Betsey Johnson: Honor for a Life of Celebrating Youth.* The New York Times.

(9) Staff writer. (October 20, 2018). *Quoted: Anderson Cooper on His CIA Internship.* The Washington Post.

(10) Radar Staff. (Oct. 27, 2008). *Anderson Cooper's CIA Secret.* Radar Online.

Chapter 20 – Mentors Worth a Million

(1) Podcast. (March 15, 2018). *Nazik Kambar.* College Success Arizona.

(2) Rutledge, M. staff writer. (Jan. 17, 2019*). 'Keep an Open Mind About What's Possible': Hamilton Native Who Rose from Poor Badin Student Donates $1M to College.* Dayton Daily News.

(3) Hern, A. (Feb. 9, 2018). *Elon Musk: The Real-Life Iron Man.* The Guardian.

(4) Vance, A. (June 5, 2015). *Elon Musk: The College Years.* Esquire.

(5) Mejia, Z. and Elkins, K. (Sept. 29, 2017). *Warren Buffett Credits His Success to These Three People.* CNBC Make It.

(6) HBO Documentary Films. (2017). *Becoming Warren Buffett.*

Chapter 21 – When All Else Fails, Work Hard

(1) Inside Edition. YouTube. (Nov. 28, 2017). *How Deborah Norville's Most Memorable Story Put Her Behind Bars.*

(2) Armour, V. (April 28, 2011) *Zero to Breakthrough: 7-Step, Battle-Tested Method for Accomplishing Goals that Matter,* pg. 23-25. Penguin Group (USA), LLC.

(3) Hardy, K. (Jan.10, 2018). Iowan Who Invented Shock Collar for Pigs Named Entrepreneur of the Year." Des Moines Register.

Chapter 22 – Keys to Launching a Great Life

(1) Achor, S. (2010). *The Happiness Advantage*, pg. 176. Random House, LLC.

(2) Hart Research Associates, (Jan. 20, 2015) *Falling Short? College Learning and Career Success*. Hart Research Associates.

(3) Clear, J. (2018). *Atomic Habits*, Page 15. Penguin Group (USA), LLC.

INDEX

Book Discussion Guide

Intro & Chapter 1:

1. How do you define success (financial, relational, career, purpose)? Would you call yourself successful? Why or why not? Who is the most famous person you have ever met? Who is the most successful person you know?

2. If you attended college, what was your major? Are you working in the field of your major? Very few people end up working in the area in which they got their degree. Why do you think that is the case?

Chapters 2, 3 & 4:

3. If you went to college, what was the best thing you got out of your experience there? If you did not go to college, what do you wish you could have access to that college provides? If you are currently en-rolled in college what do you hope to get out of it?

4. Do you agree with the statement that "having no plan is a plan to fail?" Why or why not?

5. What was one person, event or circumstance that changed your life? Did it move you to a better place or a worse place? If worse, discuss how you could "rewrite" the results of that moment to change your life for the better.

Chapters 5 & 6:

6. If you could spend the day with one famous or not-so-famous currently living person, who would it be? What would you hope to learn from them and how might it impact your life?

7. Do you have a system for remembering the names and faces of the people you meet? How do you think using a system might be beneficial you?

Chapters 7 & 8:

8. Were you addicted to getting A's while you were in school? Do you have regrets like Bill Gates about missing out on other opportunities or adventures?

9. Do you think that having a sense of humor makes a difference in one's life? Stretch your own creativity with this improv exercise: Imagine a red brick in your hands. Talk about all the different ways you could use it. (What if you ground it up?) Try this exercise with other objects to stretch your imagination.

Chapters 9 & 10:

10. Everyone has moments in their life where they believe they may have missed an opportunity. What is an opportunity you would like to explore? Who is someone you need to get to know better?

11. Do you think it is ever a good idea for a young person to turn down millions of dollars like Missy Franklin or Zach Allen did to attend college? Why? If you were given $100,000 dollars to create a business, what would you do with it?

Chapters 11, 12 & 13:

12. Who in your life has pushed you to be better? What did they want you to do?

13. To be successful you must able to challenge yourself to accomplish more than you dreamed possible. What is an exceptionally high goal that you would like to attain?

Chapter 14, 15 & 16:

14. Imagine that you had a magic wand you could wave to solve or change one thing. What would you change (other than something about yourself)? How would you do it?

15. Is there a business you have always wanted to create? If you needed a team to make it happen, who do you know that might have a similar passion and want to join you in your endeavor? If you don't know anyone, how could you find them?

Chapter 17:

16. What is the worst job or volunteer project you have ever done? What was your most interesting assignment? Where would you like to volunteer and what would you want to be doing?

Chapter 18:

17. Have you ever wanted to accomplish something big and someone told you that you could not do it? How did you move past that or did it stop you? What is your current dream project?

Chapter 19, 20, & 21:

18. If you were to do an internship at a major company, where would you like to work for a summer? What would you like to do for them?

19. Who do you turn to for financial, relational or business advice or mentoring? What is the best advice you have ever been given by someone? What book have you read that made a difference in your life? Recommend at least one book to the others in your group.

Chapter 22:

20. Choose just one thing (D.O.T.) from the last chapter to do this week. Share which one you plan to do or pursue. How will you do it? What are your fears or concerns on how to proceed? What is holding you back? Ask anyone in the group if they have suggestions on how you can begin.

Lindy Schneider and **Tom L. Schneider** are authors, speakers and coaches. They have guided thousands of college students through some of the toughest decisions of their lives as college advisors for over 16 years. They are the co-creators of *College Superhero Secrets*, a life and career success mentorship program that gives students the tools to establish great relationships and launch their careers while still in college.

Lindy and Tom have been featured guests on *ABC, CBS, NBC, FOX,* and the *CW*. They have been quoted in *U.S. News & World Report, INC.*, *Atlanta Business Journal*, *Huffington Post, USA Today Magazine, NBC NEWS* and many other outlets. Lindy is a contributing author to ten books in the NY Times best-selling book series, *Chicken Soup for the Soul*.

Tom is the creator of an innovative public school model that the U.S. Department of Education called, "the future of education in America." As a successful business person, Tom has won national awards for client retention and generated multi-millions of dollars in sales.

Other books by Tom L. Schneider and Lindy Schneider:

- *More Money in Tough Times: Discover the $10,000 You Never Knew You Had*
- *Cash for Creatives: Fast Money, Found Money, Free Money*
- *Starfish on the Beach* – a best-seller children's book

In Case You Missed It

As a "thank you" for purchasing this book Tom and I would like to give you a FREE *College Secrets* video training. We will reveal some of the myths you might have heard about college and offer concrete steps you should take to get the best ROI on your college investment.

You will also learn some simple steps you can take that will give you a distinct advantage over other college students and set you on the path to a happy, successful life.

If you are currently attending college, planning on attending or love someone who is in college or college bound, watch this valuable free video training. Go to:

www.AmericasCollegeAdvisors.com/FreeTraining

Connect with the Authors

We would love to hear from you. What inspired or motivated you? What do you want to learn more about? We would love to celebrate your success and your comments can help us better serve students in the future.

Email:
Feedback@AmericasCollegeAdvisors.com

Website:
AmericasCollegeAdvisors.com

https://www.facebook.com/AmericasCollegeAdvisors/

Tom L. Schneider:
Action Plans Inc – America's College Advisors

Lindy Schneider:
Action Plans Inc – America's College Advisors

@CollegeTipsBook

One final request: If you enjoyed this book, would you please leave a review on Amazon about your thoughts on the book? This helps us share these success secrets with more people so they can build their own successful lives. You will be doing us, and them, a great favor.

Thank you for your input. It is deeply appreciated.

Lindy Schneider and Tom L. Schneider